Cryst

"This is an excellent primer to op~~ ~~ ~~_~~ ~~_~~u of Crystal Healing and the wisdom the crystal kingd~~_~~ ~~_~~us! Shannon does an amazing job setting the stage for selecting the right crystal allies for you and your healing journey and how to cleanse, charge, and activate them. Most importantly, she teaches you how to establish a daily practice so you can truly, and more deeply, connect with your healing allies in expansive ways!"

—MARGARITA ALCANTARA, M.S. L.Ac., Shamanic Practitioner, Reiki Master/Teacher, Mentor, Chakra Expert, bestselling author of *Chakra Healing*

"I had the privilege of receiving an advanced reader copy of *Crystal Wisdom*. As a Somatic Psychotherapist and Yoga Therapist, I have always been interested in crystals and, throughout the years, have gathered many myself. The author opened my eyes up to a whole new world about crystals. I had no idea how much there was to learn. She has a wealth of knowledge about everything from the collection of them, their care, and their uses, and gently lays out a beautiful guide on how to use them for support in your meditation for self-awareness and grounding. I am so excited to use the crystals I have in a different way now, as well as to investigate gathering more based on my current needs. I highly recommend this book to anyone seeking deeper knowledge in this area for yourself, or especially for yoga therapists for the proper use and recommendation of crystals for their client's support in practice."

—ANN SAFFI BIASETTI, Ph.D.; LCSWR; CIAYT, Author of *Befriending Your Body: A Self-Compassionate Approach to Freeing Yourself from Disordered Eating*

"It is hard to write a short review for this book. How can one describe all the wonderful journeys this well-researched and well-written book took me on? It is a must-have for anyone interested in using crystals for spiritual growth and emotional healing. Each story delivers a meaningful lesson with clear instructions that are easy to follow. It is a soul-enriching read. Use it well."

—MARINA LANDO, M.S., Reiki Master and Teacher, Certified Aromatherapist, Published Author, HarmonyLifeReiki.com

"Over the years, I've collected many colorful and intricate crystals and numerous books on gemstone properties and identification. *Crystal Wisdom* is the first book I've found that provides personal, practical, step-by-step guidance on incorporating the energy of these beautiful crystals into daily life. Each story that Shannon shares and every practice she outlines in *Crystal Wisdom* offers readers the opportunity to dig deep into the wisdom that lives within us all and provides a map for mindfulness and self-exploration. Ultimately, these simple and accessible mindfulness practices are powerful tools to support personal transformation with a little help from treasures from the earth."

—JILL SOCKMAN, Founder, Blue Lotus Yoga, bluelotusnc.com

"This debut book by Shannon Marie offers a simple yet powerful contemplative practice for anyone who loves gemstones and would like to learn to connect with the healing and support they offer. Shannon walks you through everything you need to know to change your life with Crystal Wisdom: how to choose the right crystals to work with, how to clean and charge them, how to connect with your own intuition, using the gemstones as catalysts for spiritual growth, and more. Best of all, this book is down-to-earth and practical, giving you tested tools for recognizing and working through the challenges in your life so that anyone who's willing to invest the time to learn and practice the meditations described in the book will benefit from what they learn about themselves. Whether you're already working with gemstones or you're curious and ready to start, you owe it to yourself to add this book to your library and the Crystal Wisdom practice to your life."

—CLAIRE VILLARREAL, Ph.D., Host of *Letting Grow* podcast,
clairevillarreal.com

SHANNON MARIE

CRYSTAL WISDOM

UNEARTHING
the POWER of
GEMSTONES

 FOR

POSITIVE LIFE CHANGE

modern wisdom
P R E S S

modern wisdom
PRESS

Modern Wisdom Press Boulder, Colorado, USA
www.modernwisdompress.com

Published 2021

Cover Design: Melinda Martin

ISBN: 978-1-7370282-0-8 (paperback), 978-1-7370282-1-5 (epub)

DISCLAIMER

*This book is dedicated to my parents, George and Dot,
for inspiring my lifelong fascination with the world of gemstones.*

CONTENTS

Introduction

If you have opened up this book, you may have heard about the idea of crystal healing, and perhaps you're intrigued by how these beautiful creations of the earth can initiate life transformation. This is a field of information that is so vast that it's hard to glean concise and practical information about how to really make a crystal healing practice work.

I own dozens of books filled to the brim with gemstone healing benefits. There are books on crystal grids, making healing jewelry, elixirs, orgonite, rituals, and oracle cards. As a gemstone and meditation educator, I have had so many clients reach out to me to share their enthusiasm and love of crystals who also really want direction about how to begin a crystal healing practice. They've collected all these amazing stones and they really want to receive the benefits of crystal energy, but they just don't know where to turn. They sit before me with their collection, their box of beautiful crystals, and they wonder, "What's next?"

They ask this question because they know they want something to change. Life is challenging—there is no doubt about that. We are inundated with responsibilities, challenges, disappointments, hopes, dreams, grief, and even pain. It isn't even just one challenge at a time. Our days present multiple emotions, tasks, and puzzles all falling on our shoulders at once. Life can be overwhelming and often we don't have any sort of life preserver to keep us afloat. How do you manage the child who is having difficulty with school, multiple projects that need your attention, the health of your spouse and, to top it off, a flat tire? All in one day.

When we are so inundated with life stressors, days can go by in which we feel we are merely putting one foot in front of the other and barely getting through it. We put our head down and push through the challenges only to sleep poorly that night and wake up again the next day to do it again. We hardly notice the days pass or the milestones we rush by and we break down when it just becomes too much.

It doesn't have to be this way.

There is a way to sit with each of these challenges and respond with heartfelt intention. To have a life preserver to hold onto to give us some space to breathe and take a look at our current situation. To sit with our feelings and truly experience them without pushing them away. There is room for a few minutes of self-reflection and compassion to take care of yourself before you respond to the next thing that life is throwing at you.

The practices in this book will help you notice and acknowledge when current life situations need your attention and support. Crystal Wisdom is about taking some time to stop, look at our experience, figure out what our heart and soul really need, and then give it to ourselves. It's a proven method to work *with* our life events rather than struggling against them, trying to make them go away, or sweeping them under the rug. We can absolutely reduce the suffering in our lives and develop more peace through understanding the healing power of crystals and how to use them.

Initially, I thought this practice was just for me—that I had tapped into something that worked for me but might not resonate with other people. I slowly started to share videos about crystals online and soon gathered a community of people who all shared the desire to be happy and to be able to handle our daily life in a less chaotic way. They loved gemstones just as much as I do and were ready to make changes in their lives.

I heard almost daily, "This is just the information I needed today!" or "I just bought this stone and your video posted!" It was all synchronicity. Each and every viewer, client email, and video comment reinforced the idea that people wanted more from life and that gemstones were the key for us all. So many people adore gemstones but haven't found that right resource to show them how to effectively use them as a personal, spiritual, and developmental practice. This book will provide that. I hope you refer to it often and that it becomes a beloved resource that you come back to over and over and share with friends.

This book was inspired by my online community and I write it for all of you. For Kelly, who has just recently fallen in love with gemstones and just can't get enough of learning about them. To Suri, who has an enormous collection and wants to use them more formally and deliberately. To Justin, who has felt amazing transformation since meditating with gemstones and wants to take his practice even further. The people I work with want to know themselves better, live more fulfilling lives, and respond to life situations in a more confident and less stressful way. Together, we can take this journey.

CHAPTER 1

Discovering Your
Inner Crystal Guide

I imagine, dear reader, that you've already been captivated by the beauty of crystals and gemstones. Maybe you've found yourself in rock shops picking up and holding piece after piece. You've looked at all the colors, shapes, textures, and shimmers and been drawn in by their magic. Gemstones are a joy to look at, to hold, and to collect. Maybe you've indulged, purchased a whole bunch of crystals, and eagerly brought them home so you could look at each one in-depth. You hold each one up to the light and watch how the color changes, shimmers, or flashes. You see how each stone has a unique color pattern, shape, or texture. Each is a fascinating exploration.

I've often found myself in gem stores for hours and come out with bags of stones in every color I could imagine. I adore the endless variety of colors, shine, and sparkle, and even the roughness of raw stones. You can buy gemstones in their rough, natural glory or stones that are carved into any shape—such as a sphere, obelisk, or free-form—to highlight their shine, flash, and color combinations. There are smooth tumbled stones and flat palm stones to tuck comfortably in your hand. You can find huge crystal clusters and geodes that have been cracked open to display the treasure within. The variety of crystals and gemstones is wide and you can get mesmerized during your shopping experience. This may sound like a familiar experience to you if you have also discovered a fascination with gemstones.

Discovering your attraction to crystals and gemstones is the first step to unearthing a more mindful, intentional, and satisfying life. Gemstones are a key to identifying what we need more of in life, what we need to heal, and what we should pursue. They can help us to cultivate more love for ourselves and others. The crystals and gemstones we are attracted to reveal the truth we are so eagerly seeking. They bridge the gap between daily life and our innate wisdom. Gemstones have the power to help us manifest lasting life change.

But if you've searched for crystal healing resources, it may have left you overwhelmed and confused. There is a lot of information out there, but where to even begin? How does it work? What stones should I buy to help me? What do I need to do with the stones? How do I tap into these healing powers? How do I know if it's working? These are all questions I've received from my hundreds of clients time and time again. If this world of crystal healing seems confusing, it's because it is. But there *is* an easy way to tap into the wisdom of gemstones that will help you improve your life.

Illuminating the Gemstone Path

You don't need any prior experience with crystals or energy work to learn the practice I will teach you in this book, which I developed over time and have been using in my own daily life for years. It didn't come to me all at once. I began swimming in the sea of crystal healing resources. These books are as beautiful as the gemstones themselves and full of healing knowledge. The vast amount of crystal books available is a testament to the large number of people who have discovered healing and transformation using gemstones.

I absorbed the information within the pages (this was *before* the world of online videos!) and slowly began to develop my own relationship with crystals. Day in and day out, I kept sitting with my gemstones and I found an excellent personal practice that helps support me during my everyday life situations. The Crystal Wisdom practice helps me be more compassionate and mindful in my reactions (to myself and others), recognize and acknowledge when stress is happening, and sit and listen for my own wisdom to speak to me and tell me what I need. I offer it to you now in the pages of this book.

This book is not about crystal healing, but something much more intimate and life-changing—Crystal Wisdom. This practice uses gemstones to tap into your own inner wisdom and intuition to discover what you truly need and desire in life. It's about really getting to know yourself in an honest and authentic way. Crystal Wisdom is a practice of unearthing *you*. Once you know your most common life challenges, you can use gemstones to change the way you respond.

In the next chapters of the book, I will guide you step by step through the world of Crystal Wisdom in a practical and understandable way. The most common question I receive—and really, the most fundamental—is "How does it actually work?" I will help you identify the most supportive gemstones for your current life situations. This can be the most challenging part because there are just so many gemstones. We'll discuss how to buy the stones you will connect with the most and how to benefit from them. Next, we'll talk about preparing your stones after bringing them home and getting ready for the practices. Finally, I'll teach the heart of the Crystal Wisdom practice. You'll learn how to design and perform your own gemstone practices that are relevant to your life. It is so much easier than it ever has been. Imagine being able to hold, use, and connect with your crystal collection daily and have more fulfilling, satisfying days.

Your attraction to gemstones and the fact that you're reading this book prove that you are ready to bring about positive and transformative changes in your life. You only need to read on and I will be there with you, guiding you through each activity until you're actively practicing Crystal Wisdom and living a better life.

The Next Steps on Your Journey

Before we dive in, I want to simplify the terminology used for the gemstones you'll be learning about. There is often confusion regarding the use of the terms "crystals," "gemstones," "rocks," "stones," and "minerals." According to *Gemstones of the World* by Walter Schumann, "most gemstones are minerals," with some exceptions like amber, coral, and pearls. He also states, "Nearly all minerals grow in certain crystal forms." But not all crystals in nature are gemstones, such as salt, sugar, and ice crystals. A "rock" is a gemstone that is made up of more than one mineral. The term "stone" is used differently depending on the industry in which it is used. For simplicity's sake, I will be using the words "gemstone" and "crystal" interchangeably.

As you proceed through this book, you'll learn how I developed this practice, the importance of connecting with your own inherent wisdom, and how to use gemstones to trigger deep and meaningful life transformation. I invite you to sit back with this book and your favorite comforting beverage to take the next step on your journey to a more satisfying life!

CHAPTER 2

My Gemstone Journey

Everyone comes to their fascination with gemstones through their own unique experiences. I grew up hunting gemstones with my parents on the Oregon coast. That stretch of land birthed a lifelong love of gemstones that has grown and developed over time. We often went camping and, during those trips in Oregon, we would rock hunt. We would search for rocks on the coast and the desert, rivers, and forest. We always came back with at least one big bucket of gemstones every trip. My dad would transfer those stones into the rock tumbler in the garage. Each week, he would show me how to wash and prep the tumbler. I got to see this beautiful transformation of rough rocks into smooth, shiny, polished treasures. Eventually, we accumulated so many polished gemstones that we filled our flower beds with them. On rare sunny days in Oregon, the light would shine on the rocks and the whole flower bed would sparkle. Those memories are embedded deep within my heart. I thank my parents every day for introducing me to the transformational key to my life purpose.

This love of gemstones remained with me through my early adult years. I would pick up random rocks wherever I would travel. I kept my eyes open for one that stood out. It might be on a trail, in a park, or even on the road. The rock was a symbol of the memories I had of the trip. They were all kept in a special travel memories box for me to open up and enjoy the memories of places I had been.

Eventually, my collection grew so large that I needed to do something with the stones. I had no room for more. I started making jewelry out of them, wrapping them in sterling silver wire, charging them with healing Reiki energy and selling them on eBay. This gave me an opportunity to continue collecting the gemstones but without accumulating them in my house. I would create something unique with each gemstone, take a picture, and send them on to a new home. It was such a satisfying cycle.

As my gemstone business grew, I spent time collecting more wisdom and knowledge of my spiritual experience. Starting in my twenties, lasting well over a decade, I immersed myself in training, certifications, and college studies. I yearned to figure out what to do with my life. I was working a steady job at a global corporation, but it was achingly unsatisfying. I wanted to grow and develop as a person, a human being, and as an infinite soul. I was searching for that something I felt was missing. I wanted to find that one thing that would guide and steer my life, give it purpose, and enable me to lift the energy of the world. A pretty lofty goal, right?

I completed a Reiki Master and Teacher certification. This taught me how to sense and channel energy. I studied yoga and how we can work through emotions via bodywork. I learned all about the chakra system and the importance of reading the language of colors. I completed yoga teacher training and a practitioner certification with Phoenix Rising Yoga Therapy. This taught me how to hold space and facilitate a person's access to their inner body wisdom.

I received my master's degree in Transpersonal Psychology, which is the study of how spiritual and religious practices support our psychological health. I also studied meditation and Buddhist practices with my teachers at Dawn Mountain, a Tibetan Buddhist practice and research center. I was becoming more and more attuned with how meditation, intention, and honest inner exploration can bring about real transformative change in my life.

I went so far as to study gemology and received my Professional Gemologist certification. I wanted to know all aspects of gemstones—every little bit of information. I learned how to study their properties, look at them under microscopes, and identify unlabeled gemstones through the formal testing process. It was a deep dive into the world of gemstones. I learned how they are created in the earth, how light shines through them, influences how we see the color, what internal inclusions are common, and how to identify man-made gems. I had never felt so connected to my gemstone practice.

During the years of managing my jewelry-making business, I started accumulating information about the stones' supportive benefits. I included this information in the eBay listings. People appreciated being able to buy gemstone jewelry for love, patience, confidence, or any attribute they wanted to support in their life. Over time, I found that I was experiencing those benefits myself every time I worked with a stone. I found myself drawn to certain gemstones and would pick up some stones more often than others. I began to see how sitting and taking quiet time with gemstones helped me sort through stressors, problems, and emotions in my life. This was when I truly started developing my personal gemstone healing practice. I would intentionally pick stones that I knew could support what was happening in my life at that time. Stressing out at work? Howlite. Needing to clear the negativity of coworkers after a day in a cubicle? Black Tourmaline. Needing a boost of confidence? Citrine. I would keep a selection of stones with me to use whenever I needed them. It was so casual at the time that I didn't realize that it was becoming the basis for my own formal spiritual practice.

There was a moment when I had spent all day working on spreadsheets for my corporate job. The day ended and I felt so scattered and unfocused. I still had to pick up the kids from school, sit them down with homework, make dinner, and then get through after-dinner chores. Hematite immediately came to mind, so I went to my shelf to get it. It is the "stone of the mind" and helps improve grounding and focus. I sat with this Hematite, knowing that I wanted to feel more centered and focused. Just a few minutes later, I felt present, focused, and all of the effects of "spreadsheet brain" were gone. That's when I knew I needed to make more time for intentional meditation with gemstones when I needed to manage some aspect of my life.

Eventually, I started a YouTube channel dedicated to gemstone education called Reiki Gem Wellness. I wanted to start sharing bits of my learning with others. I loved rediscovering each gemstone's beauty and wisdom when creating the informational video and the guided meditation. I enjoyed answering everyone's questions and I really loved helping people start their own gemstone exploration process. I intended to truly bring the power of gemstones into the practical everyday lives of people. Knowing that Tiger's Eye increased confidence was great, but I wanted people to know when and how to use it; to see where they needed support in real-life situations, and then take action to pick up a stone and reflect on that part of their life.

I came up with my own method to figure out which crystals I needed to have readily available at home and in my purse whenever I had to go out. I chose several life stressors and development areas and the crystals to support them. Making a point to recognize when those identified situations started happening, I would pause, get the stone, and sit with it while reflecting on the emotion or situation. Rather than rushing through the challenges in the quickest way possible, I was working with and resolving my stressors. This started to change how I was living my life and interacting with other people. I was no longer reacting out of frustration or fear or waiting for the stress to simply go away. Instead, I was actively developing patience and confidence.

I realized that the gemstones weren't creating the change—I was enabling the change and the gemstones helped me unveil the path I needed to travel. I already knew the aspects of my life that I wanted to change. Working with the crystals helped me recognize and acknowledge what I already knew. They helped me find space and time to sit with emotions and challenges that I had been avoiding. They opened a valve of inner knowledge that helped me take charge of my life. That is the beauty of Crystal Wisdom. It is life-changing and such an easy, fulfilling practice, and I'm excited to share it with you.

There came a time when I just felt like my brain was full. It was overflowing with information about gemstones, healing, meditation, and consciously caring for ourselves. My website and YouTube were great ways to channel out information, but those venues proved challenging in supporting clients with the specific information or practice they needed. It was just like that sea of crystal healing knowledge out on the internet that is difficult to navigate. I am in the middle of the ocean and where is the shore? I knew I had to start writing books. I had to compile and solidify this vast amount of knowledge into forms that would help someone actually use their gemstones for personal healing and growth.

You can start working with gemstones to start actively building the life you want to have. Throughout the next chapters, I will walk with you through the process of creating your own Crystal Wisdom practice. You will learn how to research the best stones for your current life needs, confidently buy the stones, connect with and prepare those stones for practice, and soon, you'll be sitting with stones and hearing the wisdom that is already inside of you.

CHAPTER 3

What Is Crystal Wisdom?

Gemstones Are a Key to
Unlocking Inner Wisdom

I have been asked many times why I believe in "magic crystals." Rock tumbling is a favorite hobby of mine, so I know an entire community of gemstone hobbyists and professionals. Many rock hunting, rock tumbling, and geology enthusiasts roll their eyes at the mention of crystal healing. "Rocks are just rocks. They are pretty, but they don't have magic powers."

To some extent, they are correct. There is no magic "get what you want in life without work" trick or object. That is the same with gemstones. Crystal Wisdom is different from the overall expectations about crystal healing. I *don't* just hold a crystal and suddenly discover my confidence issues are gone. Gemstones are not going to fix my problems for me. There is much more to the Crystal Wisdom practice than that.

However, that is not to say that gemstones don't have a magical and transformational effect on our lives. They absolutely can! The heart of the Crystal Wisdom practice is knowing that gemstones are used as a key to unlocking access to our own inner wisdom. They act as powerful meditation tools that allow us to look inside and dissolve the barriers blocking our access to our inner truth. You already know what you want to heal, what you want to improve, and what you want to attract more of in your life. You have this vast amount of wisdom within and gemstones help to tap into all of that wisdom, allowing you to manifest actual change in your life. The Crystal Wisdom practice you'll learn will help you access your intuition, trust yourself, and know you can face your truth, make positive change, and heal. But first, let's answer some basic questions that help set the stage for building your own transformational practice with gemstones.

What Is Gemstone Energy?

This may be one of the most common questions I receive about the Crystal Wisdom practice and the world of crystal healing. The term "energy" can mean something different to each person. Energy provides human beings with the life force vitality to move, breathe, and take action. Physical human energy in action is demonstratable as we walk, talk, and jump. Mechanical energy is also easy to observe as it lights our homes, powers vehicles, and provides heat to our homes. There is also vibrational energy at a molecular level. This is a much subtler energy that can't easily be observed with our five senses. Gemstones vibrate at a molecular level, have a unique energy that is transmitted as particles called photons and can be transferred to and affect our personal energies. Practitioners of yoga, chakra healing, Ayurveda, acupuncture, Tai chi, and Reiki (as well as many other energy practices) direct and move these subtle energies to promote optimum health and vitality.

If that sounds complicated, don't worry, this practice does not rely on your ability to sense or feel gemstone vibrational energy. In fact, when I refer to gemstone energy in this book, I am describing the emotional, mental, spiritual, and physical sensations you experience when working with a gemstone. Specifically, I am referring to the gemstone's ability to inspire a desired feeling, emotion, or mindset due to your meditation and inner reflection practice. When I talk about being able to pick up a stone and quickly receive the stone's energy, I am talking about feeling the mind, body, heart, and spirit effects of your practice. In the beginning, it takes longer to sense these effects. Still, with practice, you can call up the qualities so quickly that there is a noticeable wave of relaxation, compassion, focus, or creativity that rises within you. This description is what I mean by "feeling the energy of a gemstone." It defines a much easier way of detecting the stone's energy than trying to feel its actual vibration.

What Is Inner Wisdom?

When we open up to and start trusting our sense of intuition, we receive the gift of our inner wisdom. The term intuition refers to our sixth sense that provides us with a means of taking in additional information. It is used to describe those gut feelings and innate knowing that doesn't rely on any proof for us to believe it. It is that sense that maybe something isn't going right, that we should be cautious about something, or that someone we just met is a good person. Intuition is our ability to interpret experiences from the world around us and have a strong feeling about them without any concrete proof. You go into a store and get a strong sense that you really need to go somewhere else. You leave and minutes later, the store you left is robbed. Or there is a woman at work who seems nice, but you just can't bring yourself to like her. You find out later that she's been talking about you behind your back to other coworkers. Intuition allows us to access the knowledge buried deep within us. This is how we start to hear our inner wisdom.

We are all blessed with a wealth of information that we don't necessarily access with our thinking brain. There is a core part of ourselves that knows exactly what we need in life. It has the solution to our problems, holds the truth about what we need more of in life, knows why we are afraid, and knows how to best take care of ourselves. Unfortunately, many people are never able to hear this inner voice. Knowing our truth can be a scary journey because we may not feel ready to look at what we have been avoiding. But our inner self, our Inner Guide, loves us and cherishes us.

Your Inner Guide is the voice of your inner wisdom. We can connect with and hear our Inner Guide's messages by strengthening our sense of intuition. It is that part of the essence within you that knows what you need to live the most joyous, satisfying life. Our Inner Guide truly knows what is best for us in life; however, we often don't hear or acknowledge its guidance.

For example, I know that eating a lot of sugary food is not good for me and that I should keep it to a minimum, but I still want to eat those cookies. I'm not ready to reduce the sugar intake. It took me many years of relationships to acknowledge that all those extroverted men I was dating were not what I needed. I was attracted to the qualities in them that I felt I lacked in myself, but it wasn't until my divorce that I knew I had to take a good look at what I truly wanted in a partner and to stick to those decisions. I needed someone who didn't crave the limelight and could sit with me in quiet and stillness. I did find that man and we have a wonderful relationship.

We often erect barriers between our thinking mind and our inner wisdom. Sometimes it's because we don't trust our gut or are afraid to face the answers. At other times, we don't believe our intuition because we just don't have confidence in ourselves or because we are looking for proof first. Maybe we feel we make bad choices and so we can't trust what we know inside. Believe me, looking at the truth may be scary at first, but it holds a vast treasure that can dramatically improve your life. You may not want to think about that bad breakup last year because you're afraid you'll perceive it as all your fault, but your inner wisdom wants to show you what type of relationship you really should be pursuing. Sometimes, to find our way to a better life, we have to look at those dark shadows and see the light that is just beyond it. The practice of receiving inner wisdom is a slow, steady journey of easing down those barriers, trusting ourselves to know what we need, and allowing that voice to be heard.

The Signs and Messages of Our Inner Wisdom

Our Inner Guide is begging to be heard. It provides us with information even if we aren't listening or seeking inner guidance. Our Inner Guide is not offended that we don't listen to it. This voice is persistent in its desire for us to live our fullest, most satisfying life. It is constantly whispering to us in the form of synchronicities, repeat messages, and in what we are attracted to.

Synchronicities are those times when we find a significant connection between two different events in a short period of time. Have you been thinking of a close friend you haven't seen in a while only to receive a call from them shortly afterward? I remember one day when I had been thinking of starting up my yoga practice again. I kept wondering if I should practice at home or try to find a studio, but I couldn't decide. That day at lunch, with no prompting from me, my friend told me that she had recently started yoga at a nearby studio and she thought I would love it. It turns out that was the studio where I would eventually take my yoga teacher training. Inner wisdom isn't limited to what our brain knows, but it rises when there is an upcoming opportunity that we should really take seriously.

Repeat signs and messages work the same way. While I was pregnant with our first child, my husband and I were trying to decide what to name him. We had an entire list of names but didn't feel called to any particular one. Soon, we took a trip out of town and were inundated with one name over and over and over again. We saw a city name, street name, an event flyer, a print advertisement, heard it on the radio, and someone had a child by that name at the event we were attending. We just took it as a sign that it was meant to be his name and it just felt right.

We notice things over and over again because our Inner Guide wants us to receive a message. Some people repeatedly see double or triple digits, such as 111, 222, 333, and so on. This phenomenon is a practice referred to as angel numbers, a subset of numerology, that describes how angel guides send us direct messages via repeated number sequences. The intent of the angel number message can reassure us that we will be okay, that we are supported, or that the choice we are making is the right one, depending on the number combination.

Inner wisdom also presents itself with repeated sightings of animals. This year, our yard has been overrun with lizards. I would see them any time I was out in the yard. They would often crawl across a window I was looking out and played in the bushes outside the windows. I finally looked up the meaning of lizard signs and I found that they indicate the ability to use our imagination to make something new. I was immediately struck with the realization that this was the theme of my entire year. Seeing the lizards reminded me of the importance of creativity in my life at that time. Where do you see repeat signs in your life? Do you see the shape of hearts everywhere? Or the same color car more frequently than others? You might explore the deeper meaning of these repeated signs for yourself by journaling on the topic. Each person has a different interpretation of what signs mean to them. We are subconsciously attracted to things that show us the truth and provide the information we need to find direction. If you are attracted to a particular symbol, such as a heart, your Inner Guide may be telling you that some aspect of love is crucial to you at that time. Are you looking for love? Do you feel the need to have more compassion? Do you feel unloved?

The labyrinth is a very powerful symbol for me. When I start unconsciously surrounding myself with labyrinth images, I know that I need to pay attention to my intuition and inner wisdom. The labyrinth leads us to the center, to the heart of the matter. When I need that quality in my life, I start noticing that I have brought more of that symbol into my home and meditation area. We may be attracted to a particular deity, animal, color, music, or gemstone. Looking deeper into why we surround ourselves with an object or energy can tell us vital information about what we should address in our lives. This is precisely how it works with gemstones and we can make this a powerful and intentional practice.

The History of Sacred Gemstones

All over the world and throughout time, crystals and gemstones have been prized for more than their color and sparkle. Many cultures recognized the healing, therapeutic, and spiritual properties of gemstones and included them in remedies and spiritual practices. Ancient texts and tombs help us understand how cultures used crystals for medical and spiritual purposes.

The ancient Egyptians honored a variety of stones. Lapis was a stone of royalty and used to increase personal power, while Malachite would bring clear vision and insight. Topaz symbolized the power of the Sun God, Ra, and Jade guided souls through the underworld. Bloodstone was used to cure tumors and blood ailments.

Chinese Emperor Shen Nung wrote a book over 5,000 years ago describing the effects of gemstones on the body. Chinese culture also reveres Jade for healing, prosperity, and luck, while prizing emerald for memory, intellect, and fortune-telling.

There are over 200 references to gemstones in the Bible. Exodus tells of High Priests wearing 12 gemstones, representing the 12 tribes of Israel, on their breastplates to help them connect with the Divine. John in Revelations describes a heavenly city comprised of gems. The 12 layers of the city were built with 12 different gems. Bishops often wear Amethyst rings to represent "heavenly understanding."

In England during the Middle Ages, the population used to wear stones wrapped in twine upon the body as a talisman against evil and illness. Sumerians also wore gems in a leather pouch around the neck for the same reason.

Many historical texts have been written about the therapeutic properties of stones. Aristotle spoke about the healing power of stones. Marbod, Bishop of Renens (1035-1123), wrote a book, *Liber Lapidum seu De Gemmis,* highlighting the healing properties of 60 different stones. Saint Hildegard von Bingen (1098-1179) wrote about healing practices using precious gemstones in her book *Physika*. Paracelsus (1493-1541), a physician, alchemist, and botanist, wrote *On Minerals,* focusing on the health benefits of gems and minerals. He is known for discovering medicinal uses for zinc and inventing laudanum.

Many other cultures and traditions included gemstones for healing and rituals. For example, Indian Ayurvedic medicine would prescribe elixirs, pastes, and powders made from gems. American Indians commonly use turquoise and silver in medicine rituals. Hawaiian priests (kahuna) used stones to store their mana (energy). Ancient Incas and Aztecs prized emerald as a holy stone. Australian aborigines painted rocks with sacred designs to connect with The Source and assist with dreamtime journeying.

The Supportive Properties of Gemstones

The historical uses of gemstones have been compiled into countless books over time, including references from many cultures and time periods. This is one reason why there may be many supportive qualities attributed to one stone because different cultures used it in different ways.

Stones have acquired meanings based on what the visual qualities of the stone can represent. For example, the sharp cutting edge of Obsidian has come to signify cutting attachments in one's life. The stripes and patterns on Bumblebee Jasper can represent paths or options available to us. Orbs and eye shapes on a gemstone, like Kambaba Jasper, can symbolize wheels, turning cycles, and timing. The flash and shine of Tiger's Eye and Sunstone represent the sun's bright, shining nature.

As more and more people work with gemstones, they report similar feelings and sensations when they sit with the stone. All of the qualities have been collected and compiled in the many books on crystal healing. The supportive qualities that I describe in this book have come from many different crystal healing texts. All of my favorite crystal properties books are listed in the Additional Resources section at the end of the book. I have personally sat in meditation with the gemstones and agree that the properties listed in the books help those areas of my life.

It's important to note that gemstones *represent* these qualities in our lives. They do not magically grant us these abilities. In the Crystal Wisdom practice, you will be using a gemstone to represent a particular aspect of your life. The gemstone acts as a trigger and symbol that will enable you to explore that aspect and relate to it in your life.

Using Gemstones to Hear Inner Wisdom

Now that you see how gemstones have served as powerful healing symbols throughout history, imagine if you looked for occurrences of synchronicity, repetition, and attraction via gemstones? What if you took the time to listen to your inner wisdom through your love of crystals? This is the heart of the Crystal Wisdom practice. Are you excited to hear the messages from the crystals you are drawn to?

Sitting with gemstones is a practice of self-discovery. The gemstone is the trigger of our intuition, the key, the focus point. The reason we are attracted to certain gemstones, or specific colors, is because our intuition is already guiding us. When we find that we're drawn to a particular gemstone, keep picking it up, and maybe even feel better when we do, it's because our Inner Guide is trying to tell us something.

Just recently, I found myself picking up Rhodonite on a frequent basis. It is a lovely pink and black gem that I call the Stone of Enduring Love. I found myself thinking about a piece that I have and I took it out of my crystal collection box. Feelings of anxiety plagued me for days and holding Rhodonite just helped me feel at peace. I would pick it up without thinking and rub it between my fingers. Then I realized that Rhodonite was trying to tell me something and I needed to listen. I sat down in a quiet space and held the stone. I settled, relaxed, and exhaled away my desire to "figure it out." (We'll talk more about this technique later in the book.) Then it occurred to me.

It was the week before the 2020 presidential election. Friends and family had been arguing over who should be president. Tensions and emotions were running so high and I found myself disagreeing with friends about their choice. Rhodonite helps us to love even when it is difficult. It enables us to remember why we love these people and to focus on the core of that love and compassion. I had been having such a hard time loving. I knew this, my Inner Guide knew this, and it kept bringing me back to Rhodonite as a sign to look deeper. This dramatically changed the course of that week for me. I was able to look past the politics and back at this person with compassion and empathy. I was no longer so defensive and combative. When I did feel moments of tension, I sat back down with the Rhodonite to connect back to my heart space.

Take a good look at the gemstones that you are currently attracted to. They are trying to tell you something important that you should address. I will be taking you through this exercise in detail in Chapter 4, "Guardian Gemstones". You may want to make a list now of those crystals so that you have a head start on that step.

Inner wisdom also appears to us through color. The colors we are attracted to can potentially tell us important information about what we genuinely want to cultivate in life. You might find yourself attracted to yellow. You notice all things yellow, wear yellow clothes, buy yellow flowers, paint the walls yellow, and most likely, enjoy yellow gemstones. It could be because your inner healer is telling you that you should address areas of motivation, confidence, power, and abundance in your life. It could mean that you want a pick-me-up and some more fire and enthusiasm in your days. Color attraction is an incredibly informative language within our inner wisdom.

This information comes directly from Color Psychology, which is the study of the effects that colors have on our mental and emotional well-being. Karen Haller explains in her book, *The Little Book of Colour: How to Use the Psychology of Colour to Transform Your Life*, that the study of color dates back to 490 BC with the philosopher Empedocles. Our reaction to color stems from three primary areas of input: a personal association to color (we link a color to a memory or something we like, such as a sports team), the cultural or symbolic meaning (meaning imbued by a collective cultural belief), and the psychological meaning (instinctive reactions to a color like red meaning "warning!").

I will add that colors have also developed supportive properties based on the associated colors and meanings in the chakra system, our bodies' energetic system. Each chakra represents an energy center in our energetic body. This energy center governs how we function in a particular area of our life and each center is linked to a color. For example, orange is the color of the sacral chakra. This chakra governs the energy of creativity, pleasure, and sexual reproduction in our lives. When you notice a color repeatedly, then take a moment to see if it is a message from your Inner Guide. You will learn more about the specific gemstone color attributes in Chapter 6.

Gemstone synchronicity is also a meaningful road sign. I see this happen so often in the comments of my YouTube channel. I post a video about Moonstone and I start seeing comments such as, "I just bought a Moonstone yesterday and now I see your video!" or "I have been having trouble with self-care and your Moonstone video just reinforced how important this is." Even, "I have Moonstone coming in the mail right now!" I recently saw a comment from a grieving woman who said, "My friend just lost her son and your video about Apache Tears was the first thing I saw on YouTube this morning." She needed help grieving and a video about just the right stone for her popped into her life. It is vital to take note of synchronicities.

They are the signs from the Universe, the messages from our spirit and angel guides, and the tap on the shoulder from our Inner Guide.

Crystal Wisdom is about allowing us to intentionally open up to this inner knowing. It is about identifying those situations in life that we want support with, finding those gemstones that will support that situation, untapping the related wisdom, and using it to help us make actual change. Crystal Wisdom encourages us to examine why we are attracted to certain gemstones and colors. Can't seem to put Amethyst down? Then maybe it is time to tap into your intuition more, spend quiet time in meditation, or take time for yourself to sleep more. Look at the properties that Amethyst supports and identify why Amethyst keeps speaking to you.

Then commit to keep sitting with Amethyst and allow your own inner wisdom to rise up, see the areas in your life that it affects, and how you really feel about it. Does it elicit hesitation, fear, excitement, or enthusiasm? If so, why? Let the wisdom flow. You'll learn how to use gemstones when you need them and discover where you might be blocking your personal development, avoiding things, or not addressing emotions. Or you might be afraid of something, hiding something, or just need to cultivate more of some quality in your life. This is how we develop a relationship with Crystal Wisdom to figure out the truth within.

Actively Channeling Crystal Wisdom to Make Change

The next step in the Crystal Wisdom practice is to take some action in our lives. This is where the actual life transformation happens. Our lives don't get better just from knowing; we also need to make a change, even if it is just a change of attitude. This is where the magic happens.

Maybe you have decided you want to be more patient during frustrating situations. Then sit with a patience gemstone, such as Howlite, whenever you feel impatient. See how impatience feels to you. Where does your body feel it? What does the emotion of it feel like? What thoughts arise? Sitting and watching is the key to hearing the inner wisdom. Consider what made you so frustrated. You might find that you are triggered by a specific personality trait, a situation, or a need for control. What about those situations make you so frustrated? Once you know the trigger and why you may be triggered, you can plan how to address those situations before you are in them. You might bring Howlite with you to a frustrating meeting. Holding it will remind you of the patience you so desire. Sitting with the Howlite helps you to unlock all the wisdom you already know about your impatience. It enables you to learn from it, prepare, and make life changes. It also provides support to you during those experiences.

This worked for me when I needed support during the election week. First, I recognized that I was being called to Rhodonite. Then, I listened. I sat with the stone and let my Inner Guide tell me why I was attracted to that stone. I acknowledged that it was indeed what I was experiencing. Finally, I took action. I changed my attitude from confrontation to love. This is the transformative effect of Crystal Wisdom.

One client, Michael, was living one of the most stressful lives I could imagine. He worked as an emergency dispatcher. This job required him to spend at least eight hours a day listening to the worst moments in people's lives. He heard moments when callers were fighting, watching someone die, scared for their lives, or lost and afraid. There were times when he'd hear a person's final words. All of his coworkers experienced this stress as well and there was no counseling or outlet at work for them to manage these emotions. He would take this tension, anxiety, and sometimes despair home to his family. He felt he couldn't talk about this to his wife without making her depressed as well. It caused him to have frequent nightmares.

He asked me, "What can I do? What crystal can help me cope with my job?" I recommended carrying Black Tourmaline with him to support him in letting go of the negative and harsh energy that was building up inside and going home with him. It would encourage him to strengthen his personal energy boundaries so he could do his important work without taking on every call's emotional energy. He could sit with the stone at the end of his shift and intentionally let go of the emotional attachments before he went home. Black Tourmaline supports transmuting negative energy to positive. It encourages us to look at a situation and cultivate the positive rather than amplify the negative. Michael could then see all the good he accomplished that day to help save people, rather than the tragic circumstances that forced them to call. He could say a blessing for anyone who was lost, rather than continually ache over their passing. Michael had worked through the Crystal Wisdom steps: recognizing a change needed to happen, finding a crystal that could help support him during that specific situation, taking moments with the stone to listen to his own wisdom, and changing the way he framed his work experience. This is the transformative power of Crystal Wisdom.

This is how gemstones can change our lives. Gemstones allow us to live our lives authentically, honestly, and intuitively. Do they make life perfect? No. But they do enable us to navigate the stressors and chaos of life with more intention and mindfulness. They help us make more considered decisions and respond more mindfully to events and relationships in our lives. The practice of Crystal Wisdom ignites alchemy within us. I will show you exactly how to cultivate this alchemy in your own life in the following chapters. You don't have to have any prior experience working with gemstones. We will go through every stage together until you start to see the magic working in your life.

Preparing for Your Journey

As you ready yourself to begin this adventure, I recommend the practice of journaling to help put your experiences and feelings into words for future reflection.

Take some time to find a special journal that you can dedicate just to this practice. Allow your creative self to guide you toward a journal that speaks to you. If you don't have one already, you can plan a sacred time to purchase one. There is so much variety in colors, styles, and sizes of journals available online. If you'd prefer to see and hold them first, find a local office supply or stationery store for some shopping time. Your connection to your journal will be as strong as your relationship with your crystals and is part of your Crystal Wisdom toolkit.

As a supplement to your journal, I also have a worksheet available on my website, titled "Identifying Your Guardian Gemstones". This can be found at www.crystal-wisdom.com/crystalwisdombook. This worksheet will guide you through every step of the process of identifying the gemstones that can help you the most. I will talk more about this in Part 1, "Gathering and Preparing Your Guardian Gemstone Team". This worksheet will help you keep your discoveries in a concise, consolidated place for future reference.

The Practice of Journaling

Once you have your journal, you are ready to begin on the Crystal Wisdom journey. This journal will help you from the very beginning as you choose your gemstones to the later stages when you are developing and sitting in daily meditations.

Why is journaling so important? The act of writing down your inner wisdom will enable you to make the inner wisdom messages concrete. You acknowledge that you received the information from your Inner Guide and are documenting it for further reflection. Journal entries will help you uncover the root source of life challenges, discover patterns of thoughts and behaviors that are causing stress and complications in life, and unveil your authentic life goals and dreams. It is vital to the act of manifesting change in your life.

Your journal is where you will document all experiences with your Crystal Wisdom practice. This could include the notes you take and the gemstones you select during Part 1, "Gathering and Preparing Your Guardian Gemstone Team". It could also be where you record the synchronicities and repeat messages you notice during the day.

There is no definitive and correct way to journal, but I will provide some examples in Chapter 11, "Building Your Daily Practice". Do not feel limited as to what you should or shouldn't write in your journal. Write down whatever impressions, messages, images, felt sensations, or emotions arise for you. You can draw pictures, write poems, or express wisdom as it is emerging for you. Describe your life challenges and how you felt about them that day. This will be where you start to see how your reaction and feelings about life situations begin to change. As you read over your past journal entries, you will be able to notice progress, perhaps that a particular heartache doesn't feel as intense anymore, or that it's feeling more natural to speak in public, or that you are more patient in frustrating circumstances. The transformation will take shape and come to life the more you practice and you will be able to witness it within the pages of your journal.

PART I

Your Crystal Wisdom Practice

Gathering & Preparing
Your Guardian Gemstone Team

CHAPTER 4

Guardian Gemstones

During the first few steps of our Crystal Wisdom journey, you will be identifying your Guardian Gemstones. As much as you may be in love with the gemstones you may have, whether you've got a handful or a sizeable collection, I find that you don't need to work actively with all of them all of the time. That would get overwhelming and you wouldn't see any significant improvement in your life. In fact, it may even cause more stress and pressure. As you work through this book, I will guide you through identifying a small team of crystals to build an intentional, focused practice around. These are called Guardian Gemstones.

These gems will act as keys to unlock your inner wisdom and change your life. Guardian Gemstones are those gems that will support you during identified, current life situations. This set of crystals will become your team of guides and protectors and a source of comfort during your process of inner exploration and daily meditations. The guardians will be there for you whenever you need help.

I recommend choosing anywhere from three to six gemstones to support you in some way. This range is something that I have narrowed in on through my own work, as well as my clients' work with this practice. With more than six stones, the practice may start to feel overwhelming and hard to maintain.

This group of crystals will be your primary set of Crystal Wisdom stones to help with current life situations. You will learn many ways to identify your Guardian Gemstones. If you end up with more than six in your initial list, I recommend choosing the top six focus areas and reserving the remaining gemstones for future practice.

Having a Guardian Gemstone team does not invalidate the other gemstones you may own. Your team will evolve over time as your life challenges and goals change. Any additional gemstones you may own could very well become part of your team in the future. When you are well established and comfortable with your Crystal Wisdom practice, you can even create secondary Guardian Gemstone teams to assist with other projects and life challenges. Having a more extensive collection of gemstones can be very useful for adapting to life changes over time. Still, for the purposes of this Crystal Wisdom practice, I will focus primarily on working with one primary Guardian Gemstone team.

How are Guardian Gemstones Chosen?

The essence of starting the Crystal Wisdom practice requires that you take a good look at your life and what gems and colors continue to appear in your life in order to narrow down the life issues for which you want support. If you're going to create change in your life, you need to identify specific situations for which you want help. If you don't acknowledge that you need assistance, or own the challenges you are having, then the healing process cannot begin. Create the intention and motivation to do the work that will bring about change. The life challenges you select will then narrow down the choice of your Guardian Gemstones. The crystals will help you build the energy and mindset to handle anything that life brings you.

I currently have a Guardian team that is supporting me while writing this book. While Carnelian helps boost creativity and allows new ideas to arise, Sodalite encourages me to channel my authentic truth and voice as I write. Hematite helps me choose the best words for my message. Finally, Apatite strengthens the reception of my inner wisdom and allows me to translate it into a message to share. This book will guide you step by step through the process of building your optimal Guardian Gemstone team explicitly designed for your life challenges.

In this next section of the book, I'll guide you through examining current life challenges and matching gemstones that can support you. You'll then reflect on which gemstones and colors you are attracted to and figure out what that attraction means. This is a practice of listening to your inner wisdom.

You'll discover how birthstones, numerology, and astrology can also help you identify those gemstones that can affect real change in your life. It may be difficult to imagine that every Pisces is going through the same life problems. That is definitely a concept I pondered many times during my studies. I've come to learn that the themes and overall "soul goals" we face throughout our lives are revealed to us via the exact day and month of our birth. I think it's no accident that I was born exactly when I was, and I'll share how you can unearth those life themes you may not have realized were following you. This can be a powerful new way to look at and live your life journey.

Each step of the Crystal Wisdom practice is a self-exploration—an inner journey—that enables you to look at your life with openness, honesty, and vulnerability to decide what will truly make you happy. This may seem like an intimidating process at first, but I assure you that once you open up to your inner wisdom and discover your truth, as painful as it might be at first, it will guide you to the path of healing and eventual joy. If we don't acknowledge a problem and don't say it out loud, we can't change it. Remember, you don't need to tackle the huge issues first. There are plenty of smaller life situations that will welcome supportive energy. Little successes add up to significant life improvement.

Adding Guardians to Your Collection

If you don't currently have the gemstones you need in your collection, you'll learn how to find trusted gemstone sellers. I receive a vast amount of questions about how to purchase gemstones. There is an abundance of crystal sellers in brick-and-mortar stores and even more online. It can be overwhelming to start shopping if you haven't already found a favorite store. We'll talk about the buying options, how treated and synthetic stones affect a practice, and the red flags to look out for when shopping for crystals.

Once you find a seller, we'll talk about how to choose the specific piece you want to work with. Rough, polished, towers, large, small, we'll discuss it all. It's important to realize what form of stone you are attracted to because choosing just the right stones will strengthen your connection to the gemstone and practice itself. Buying future gemstones will become part of your Crystal Wisdom ritual. I think you'll find, if you haven't already, that crystal shopping can be an exhilarating hobby. Consider it an investment in your emotional, mental, and spiritual health that will also add beautiful décor to your home.

Caring for your Guardian Gemstones is also an essential part of this practice. You'll learn how to cleanse, charge, and activate your crystals. These Guardian Gemstones will form your practice's core tools and it is important to treat them as sacred objects that you cherish. The care you give to your precious collection will strengthen your connection to the stones and the intentions you set with them. The focus of each stage of the process ultimately enhances the power of the meditation practices.

Using the Guardian Gemstones When You Need Them

Once you've identified the life situations or challenges you seek support with, you will have your Guardian Gemstones nearby in a special place that is easily accessible. When you feel the situation or emotion arises, you will get the stone you identified and sit in the practice you developed. This is the most vital aspect of the Crystal Wisdom practice! Use the gemstones when you need them. Don't just let them gather dust on a shelf. Improvement won't happen only by intention and hope alone. We need to take action. The more you practice, the quicker and more potent the effects will become, until holding the stone for only moments will create a change in your emotions, energy, and physical sensations.

I will be guiding you in developing your own daily and spontaneous practices to help you tap into the energy and support of your crystal team whenever you need it to access your inner wisdom and unearth the truth that you need to hear. You will gain life-changing insights that lie at the core of the life challenge. The spontaneous practices are designed to be quick, just a few minutes whenever you feel challenged or the emotions rising.

The combination of a daily practice and a spontaneous practice will initiate the alchemy of change in your life. You'll notice your reactions to certain situations adapt and become less of a struggle. You'll find pain dissolving, attachment to habits releasing, and stress melting away. You will likely notice many more signs from the Universe showing up because you actively use your intuition and pay closer attention in life. These signs, synchronicities, and intuition impressions are also powerful information for your journal. This transformation only happens if you take the time to practice and use your Guardians regularly.

Regularly Update Your Team

Your Guardian Gemstones will evolve and change over time. This is normal and expected. As you work through life issues, they will resolve and you will no longer need daily practices for them specifically. If you find yourself using a stone less and less over time, it's an excellent opportunity to take a look at that life situation and see where it stands in your life. Are you no longer frustrated and triggered by a specific person in your life? Great! Maybe you changed jobs and no longer need support for that stressful environment. Excellent. Sometimes new challenges arise and we find ourselves in need of a new Guardian. It is a good idea to sit with the

Guardian Gemstone identification process at least every six months or when you notice a significant change in your life situations.

During 2019, I was preparing to leave my full-time job and focus on my gemstone business. This wasn't a quick process because a series of changes needed to be made to enable our family to leave that stable income behind. I needed to get the business started and plan out its future. That year, I worked with Mookaite to build the courage to make a massive change and the confidence to jump into a brand-new adventure. Kambaba Jasper helped me get in touch with my trust in divine timing and know when it was the right time to take all the small steps leading up to the final change. Charoite helped me stand calm, present, and stable during the actual transition itself.

Now the change is complete. The year 2020 brought with it a completely different set of challenges. During that challenging year, I wanted to develop the confidence to help my kids with school, stay calm yet careful during the coronavirus pandemic, and send compassion, love, and healing to all of the communities in pain. My Guardian Gemstones have evolved with me and you will learn how to read and adapt your team as well.

Also, as you get used to working with crystals in practice, you'll develop a larger capacity to work with more stones at a time. Maybe for a particular situation, you have a mini team of Guardians rather than just one. This is a practice that will expand and deepen over time with enough practice.

This is the benefit of having a larger collection of crystals with which to work. The gemstones that aren't currently on your Guardian team may very well be in the future. The more familiar you get with this process and practice, the easier it will be to choose gemstones to help you when new situations arise. Even if you just need help to get you through the week. The rest of your gemstone collection is there on standby as your life situation evolves.

As you proceed through the following chapters, take as much time as you need before moving to the next chapter. I recommend that you be present during the experience of each stage. Take time with each moment of inner exploration. Honor the truth that arises. Have compassion for yourself when it hurts. Celebrate the strengths that arise, your ability to be present, and your desire to grow. Absorb the inner wisdom that will now have a voice through your gemstone collection. I wish you a beautiful and transformative journey.

CHAPTER 5

Identifying Guardian Gemstones for a Life Situation

Which Life Situations Are Most Challenging for You?

If you want to make genuine and practical life changes, you'll need to look at your daily life and select a few situations or emotions with which you would like assistance. This is the first of a multistep process to build your team of Guardian Gemstones. Make sure to check out the worksheet, "Identifying Your Guardian Gemstones", at www.crystal-wisdom.com/crystalwisdombook. This exercise can also be recorded in a favorite journal if you prefer.

I recommend taking a half-hour to work on this exercise. Find a quiet place to sit where you can reflect and write. You may want to have a comforting drink with you, put on soft music, or light a candle. Create an environment that will help you relax and focus on listening to your inner voice. Consider the following questions concerning your life right now.

- Which areas of your life are you trying to nurture, expand, and encourage to thrive?

- Which areas of your life are causing you stress, frustration, sleeplessness, or seem to be blocking your progress in life?

- Do you have any significant decisions to make?

- Is there anything in your life that you need to release and let go of?

- Are there times when you feel you need more grounding, protection, or courage?

- Are there emotional, physical, or spiritual wounds you need to heal?

Select just three answers to start that you would like to pursue improving actively. Write these answers down in the worksheet or journal. This can be an intimidating or scary activity. You are acknowledging and giving a voice to an area of pain or need in your life. But I assure you that honoring and nurturing this space within you will lead to growth, transformation, and healing.

Keep in mind that you don't need to reserve the Crystal Wisdom practice for dramatic or extreme life problems. The situations you choose can be large or small. Remember that many small stressors can accumulate into an overwhelming situation. You also don't have to tackle the most painful or difficult challenge right at the beginning. Choose some life areas that seem manageable and will create a noticeable impact on your life if you change them. For your gemstones to act as effective lifeboats steering you to the shore, these situations need to be aspects of your life that you genuinely want to change for you. If someone else wants you to be more outgoing, well, this practice isn't for them. What do *you* want?

A client, Jennifer, wanted to be able to cultivate patience and peace when helping her kids with distance learning. Her experience with daily remote school learning felt chaotic, noisy, and highly frustrating. The coronavirus pandemic forced many parents into this role and she had not been prepared for it. The technology was new to her, the learning system had glitches, and she struggled to create a smooth daily routine. I advised her to sit with both Green Aventurine and Fluorite. Green Aventurine would help her cultivate patience and compassion for herself and her kids. With Fluorite, she would focus on developing a daily routine that would provide ease and stability to the day. She would take time daily to sit with Fluorite to plan and prepare for the next day or week. This daily time helped her begin to steer the day's events rather than allow them to drag her along. Green Aventurine was her spontaneous practice stone and she would take a few moments to sit with it when she felt frustrated or overwhelmed. The more often she used these stones, the quicker and easier these qualities would arise for her. The family's school days dramatically improved in their tone, task flow, and level of fun.

Consider the following list of everyday life scenarios to help you find a gemstone that will support your chosen life needs. It's best to select your top three so that you don't get overwhelmed as you begin your Crystal Wisdom practice:

<u>Gemstones by Life Situation</u>

- Reducing stress and anxiety: Lepidolite, Howlite, Amazonite, Moonstone

- Feeling safe and protected: Hematite, Obsidian, Black Tourmaline, Smoky Quartz

- Recovering from heartache: Rose Quartz, Rhodonite, Green Aventurine, Rhodochrosite
- Improving patience: Howlite, Green Aventurine, Emerald
- Reducing intense emotions (frustration, anger, despair): Howlite, Amazonite, Lepidolite
- Increasing confidence: Citrine, Honey Calcite, Gold Topaz, Sunstone
- Facing fears and phobias: Bloodstone, Aquamarine, Girasol Quartz
- Increasing compassion: Rose Quartz, Rhodonite, Green Aventurine, Rhodochrosite
- Inspiring creativity: Carnelian, Red Jasper, Orange Calcite, Bumblebee Jasper
- Attracting love: Ruby, Rose Quartz, Rhodochrosite
- Increasing physical passion: Ruby, Garnet, Red Jasper, Carnelian
- Boosting energy and motivation: Ruby, Garnet, Red Jasper, Carnelian
- Strengthening intuition: Amethyst, Labradorite, Lapis Lazuli, Indigo Gabbro
- Letting go of the past: Aquamarine, Apache Tears
- Easing loneliness: Snowflake Obsidian, Mookaite, Rose Quartz
- Encouraging self-care: Moonstone, Pearl, Rose Quartz
- Loss and grieving: Apache Tears, Smoky Quartz

- Making big decisions: Mookaite, Bumblebee Jasper, Kambaba Jasper, Fluorite

- Getting organized: Fluorite, Red Jasper

- Studying and learning: Fluorite, Hematite

- Starting something brand new: Mookaite, Honey Calcite, Citrine, Bumblebee Jasper

- Fertility and pregnancy: Carnelian, Orange Calcite, Rose Quartz, Unakite

- Getting better sleep: Amethyst, Howlite, Amazonite

- Cultivating relationship harmony: Amazonite, Rhodonite

- Grounding and focus: Hematite, Obsidian, Black Tourmaline, Smoky Quartz

- Encouraging relaxation and celebration: Amazonite, Dalmatian Stone, Strawberry Quartz

- Strengthening personal boundaries: Sunstone, Red Jasper, Snow Quartz, Fuschite

Once you have chosen your life situations and identified them on the list, you will notice more than one gemstone in each category. This is because all gemstones provide multiple supportive benefits. As a result, you get to select which stone you are more attracted to and then initiate the connection and energetic relationship you have with your stone. There are a couple of ways to narrow down your stone selection. You'll tap into your inner wisdom to help you decide. If you already have these stones in your collection, take them out and sit with them. To which one are you most drawn? Which one looks most interesting? When you hold it, which one feels most comfortable? Let your intuition be your guide in selecting the one stone to support that chosen life situation.

If you don't already own these crystals, there are two other ways to determine which one to use. You could go to a local gem store and do the same practice there. Hold them, sort through the selection, and see which one you are most attracted to. We will talk more about the gemstone buying process in Chapter 8. The second way is to look at pictures of the gemstones. Which one is your eye drawn to quickest? Which color do you like more? Once you have chosen the Guardian Gemstone for the three situations, you can buy them and place them aside. Later in the book, we'll talk about how you can store your sacred Guardians.

CHAPTER 6

Identifying Guardian Gemstones through Attraction

You may be drawn to individual crystals already. As you begin to select your team of Guardian Gemstones, it's important to notice which gemstones are already speaking to you. Your inner wisdom will be your primary source of input during this process. Our Inner Guide and spirit protectors talk to us through signs, symbols, songs, attraction, and repeat messages. As I mentioned previously, what we are attracted to is sending us an important message about what we want and desire. Inner wisdom is providing light to illuminate the path that will lead you to your Highest Good. In this practice, the messages are arriving in the form of crystals and gemstones.

To Which Gemstones Are You Attracted?

In your journal or worksheet, write down any gemstones to which you feel particularly drawn. Have you found yourself buying a lot of Amethyst? Are you picking up and holding the Rose Quartz often? Do you see frequent occurrences of a particular gemstone in social media? Which ones are standing out for you? If you have noticed this attraction, pick one or two of these stones and write down their names in your journal.

Do some research to discover what these gemstones support and what benefits they provide. You can look in gemstone books, internet searches, and gem stores often have this information as well. You can find an abundance of this information on my YouTube channel, www.youtube.com/c/ReikiGemWellness. Do any of the gemstone benefits stand out to you? Notice what seems to get your attention quickly. The quality that stands out may also feel very comfortable, familiar, or even a little triggering because sometimes the truth can feel uncomfortable.

For instance, if you read about Amethyst, you will find that it supports better sleep, strengthening a connection with intuition, and releasing cravings. What might quickly pop up is the difficulty you've had sleeping lately. It has been hard falling asleep, you've had nightmares, and the sleep deprivation is causing difficulty functioning during the day. This is a message from your Inner Guide that you need to focus on better sleep to improve how you're living your days. Whatever arises for you, write these notes down in your journal or worksheet. You may even discover that the stone and life situation this attraction stone supports is one that you already identified in the first exercise. You don't need to add an extra stone to your collection, but it does serve as reinforcement that your initial choice was most appropriate.

To What Colors Are You Attracted?

The next Crystal Wisdom reflection exercise is going to unveil even subtler messages from your intuition. Take about 15 minutes to sit in a quiet space. Consider any colors that you seem particularly drawn to right now. *Right now* is the key. You may have loved the color green last year or always considered purple to be your favorite color, but is it right now? Think about what color you prefer for clothing, wall hangings, pillows, markers, the covers of journals, and iPad holders. Is there one that stands out right now? If you were to choose any writing journal cover color you can imagine, what would it be? There could be more than one, so write them both down if you have a close tie.

Colors have a significant impact on our psychology and moods. There is a reason why interior decorators carefully choose color schemes for individual rooms of a house, hospital rooms, and restaurant walls. It is to encourage a feeling in the person who enters the room. Each color represents a quality to which we feel drawn. These associations come from books on color psychology, chromotherapy (healing with color), and the chakra system. After you write down your colors, read about them in the chart below.

- Black: safety and protection (Black Tourmaline, Hematite, Onyx, Smoky Quartz)

- Brown: growth, expansion, and development (Mahogany Obsidian, Petrified Wood)

- Red: passion and energy (Ruby, Red Jasper, Garnet)

- Orange: creativity and movement (Carnelian, Orange Calcite, Poppy Jasper)

- Yellow: confidence, motivation, and abundance (Citrine, Honey Calcite, Tiger's Eye)
- Green: healing and harmony (Green Aventurine, Amazonite, Emerald)
- Pink: love, compassion, and relationships (Rose Quartz, Rhodonite, Rhodochrosite)
- Blue: truth, communication, and authenticity (Sodalite, Sapphire, Kyanite)
- Light Blue: expansion, freedom, and connection with spirit (Angelite, Blue Aventurine, Celestite)
- Purple: inner wisdom and intuition (Amethyst, Stichtite, Charoite)
- White: cleansing and purity (Selenite, White Calcite, Snow Quartz)

If you find that you are surrounding yourself with one of these colors, your Inner Guide is letting you know that you should look more closely at the associated qualities in your life. Are you surrounding yourself with pinks? Where in your life does your concern about love show up? Are you seeking love? Preventing love from entering your heart? Having a hard time with a friendship? Needing more self-compassion? If you would like to further explore this aspect of yourself, then write it down in your journal and select a gemstone of that color to help support you.

CHAPTER 7

Using Your Birthday
to Guide Your Gemstone Selection

There are a number of supplemental sources to help you compile your Guardian Gemstone team based on your birthdate. You may add a stone or two to your collection based on these readings, or it may help you narrow down your choice of a gemstone for a life situation. These explorations may also just confirm the selections you have already made and provide you with some added insight. These exercises are opportunities to reflect deeply on your life experience and reveal the wisdom contained within.

I struggled with the concept of astrology and zodiac signs because I couldn't imagine that every Aries in the world is experiencing the same life challenges. Well, I found that it's not as simple as that. There is a combination of factors that contribute to the overall theme and challenges of one's life. The day, month, and year of our birth is not an accident. I believe our souls chose to be born at that specific moment for a reason. I was two weeks late, so my soul was hanging on stubbornly to reach a particular moment for birth. These factors of astrology, birthstone, and numerology can be combined to show a multidimensional view of our strengths, challenges, and life lessons experienced during this human body incarnation.

A question I often receive is, "What is the difference between birthstones and stones for zodiac signs?" Birthstones are specifically connected to the *month in which we are born*. Zodiac signs and date ranges are tied to the *constellations that were in the sky at your time of birth*. Birthstones represent the energetic influence of that month, while zodiac stones embody the constellation's energetic impact.

What Is Your Birthstone?

The first birth gemstone category we'll talk about is our birthstone. I think this is the most common and familiar birthday fact everyone knows about themselves. I was born in February, so my birthstone is Amethyst. Growing up, I collected Amethyst jewelry and was gifted it by friends and family simply because it was my birthstone. I liked Amethyst, but it wasn't until much further into my gemstone journey that I discovered the secret life messages our birthstones have to offer us. Each birthstone provides us with a glimpse at the opportunities that will arise for us repeatedly during our lives. This can be such valuable information if we identify this and learn how to actively cultivate these qualities in our lives. You may not feel connected to the birthstone theme at first and that is okay. These could be potential strengths that you may still need to develop. But once you are aware of the underlying message, you can work to make this into a powerful life strength. As you read the information listed for your birthstone, take some time to write in your journal or the worksheet from my website to identify where you might have seen occurrences of this in your life.

The following birthstone entries are made from a Northern Hemisphere experience, so I need to acknowledge the fact that the Northern and Southern Hemispheres experience the seasons at opposite times of the year. Therefore, if you live in the Southern Hemisphere, the following information about birthstones may not resonate with you due to the month names' and symbols' heavy seasonal influence.

As I was doing my research very early on in my gemstone practice, I tried very hard to find symbolism and meaning for birthstones that would be more globally inclusive. However, the Gregorian calendar and the predecessors it was based on were created in Europe. The months were named for Roman Gods and Latin phrases that represented the seasons as experienced in Europe. The birthstone system was also developed in America. The vast majority of symbolism for the calendar and the birthstone system tie them to a Northern Hemisphere seasonal experience. However, the descriptions of birthstone personality types can still apply to anyone born in that month, regardless of where they live.

January (Garnet)

January is the start of a brand-new year and a fresh cycle of life and Garnet is the Stone of Renewal. December is a month for letting go of what you no longer need and January is for starting anew! Both January and Garnet have the energy to take a new look at our life, be remotivated, and start things off on a positive note. Those born in January look for new adventures and skills and enjoy meeting new people. Novelty is a benefit because life changes don't feel like a loss but an opportunity for a new adventure. The Garnet birthstone will also provide a sense of hope during troubled times.

The Garnet soul isn't too rattled during a crisis because they are hopeful and look for the positive—the light in the dark.

Themes for January children:

- Transitioning away from things we have completed and starting anew
- Strength during life transitions
- Optimism during troubling times

February (Amethyst)

February is a winter month and touches on the winter theme of quiet, solitude, and inner reflection. We may be feeling a little housebound if the weather is harsh or rainy. Amethyst as a birthstone is very internal and expansive at the same time. Amethyst is known to awaken our intuition, deepen meditation, and support spiritual growth. Amethyst children often feel that desire to explore the inner world, just as winter causes many to retreat inside. But Amethyst does help the feelings of cabin fever as it helps us feel expansive beyond our physical body. It helps us open up to the wisdom of the Universe and enables us to feel free from physical bonds.

Amethyst is also a stone that is said to help break addictions. Those with Amethyst as a birthstone may find themselves prone to cravings and addictions—not necessarily to addictive substances, but also shopping, hobbies, relationships, etc. Amethyst helps us to release cravings by magnifying feelings of contentment and peace with what we have now.

Themes for Amethyst children:

- A recurring desire to explore the spiritual

- Being sensitive to our intuitive nature

- Cycles of cravings or addictive behaviors

March (Aquamarine and Bloodstone)

March is a month in which winter is starting to thaw and release its grip. We can get outside more because even though it may not be warm yet, it's not quite as frigid. We are saying goodbye to winter and looking forward to spring. Such is the same for Aquamarine. We are saying goodbye to the past and stepping forward into our future. We are getting outside of our comfort zone and expanding ourselves as people and souls. This is a great time for noticing opportunities if we allow ourselves to stop looking back, although it requires some confidence and courage since transitions away from what we're used to can cause some uncertainty and doubt. But this is the strength of both Aquamarine and Bloodstone: courage. The March soul has an immense reservoir of strength and courage. They know that spring and its sunshine and flowers are waiting after the winter that kept you deep inside.

Themes for Aquamarine and Bloodstone children:

- A life of stepping outside your comfort zone and expanding who you are

- Facing and releasing fears

- Learning what supports you and doesn't and releasing what is not healthy for you

April (Diamond)

April is a month of brightness and renewal as we leave winter behind and spring is blossoming. This is a time of hope, light, and new opportunities. Everything is fresh and life is blooming. There is inherent confidence and optimism in the Diamond child as they are not afraid to let their brilliance shine. These are the aspects of Diamond that are reflected in the month of April. Diamond brings light and freshness and attracts new opportunities to manifest and grow in your life. Diamond helps us transition from darkness to light, as April transitions us from winter.

Themes for Diamond children:

- A life of opportunity and true development. Don't overlook the signs and opportunities from the Universe.

- In this life, you can work on discovering your heart's desire and manifesting it into your life. But remember, it's not automatic. It will still take work, but you have the right energy to support your efforts.

- This is a life of stable, supportive relationships. But make sure that the relationships you commit to are mutually supportive—a two-way street.

May (Emerald)

Emerald is the Stone of the Heart and resonates deeply with the heart chakra. Just as the flowers bloom in the warmth of the May sun, Emerald encourages warmth and love to blossom within. The May child is a master of bringing unity, patience, compassion, and empathy to relationships. This person may be the bringer of peace during family gatherings. Have you noticed if others look to you to resolve disputes or talk to someone else on their behalf? If you find yourself struggling in life, then come back to the heart center and it will be your faithful guide. Birth and growth are abundant during the spring month of May. Emerald souls may crave large families with lots of children.

Themes for Emerald children:

- Compassion and empathy
- Balancing and harmonizing forces in relationships
- Patience and calm during the storms of life

June (Pearl and Moonstone)

This month is the very beginning of summer. It's warm, the sun is shining, and people can finally get outside. This is a time to take in the sun's rejuvenating vitamin D, relax on the beach, or in a hammock outside. People start to take vacations and recuperate after the school year is over. Pearl and Moonstone are very nurturing gemstones. They encourage you to make time for regular self-care, have a work/life balance, and rest when you need to. These are also the stones for the nurturers as they are very supportive of those in the medical profession, parents, hospice workers, and anyone in the healing field. There is a natural ability and desire to take care of others. These gemstones also encourage inner reflection, taking quiet moments to look inside and assess what we need. In June, many take a moment to pause and relax after the school year is over, the spring rain is subsiding, and the summer is starting.

Themes for June children:

- Knowing the importance of rest and self-care
- The role as the caretake or healer
- Being able to access inner wisdom for health checks

July (Ruby)

During the month of July, the sun is high and the heat is on. This is a month of heat, fire, and sweat. Ruby is the Stone of Energy and Passion and it brings heat to our lives! This gemstone encourages creativity, movement, personal drive, and passion and will often represent artists, leaders, and motivational speakers. Ruby cultivates a love of our body, movement, and having really passionate and physical relationships. The Ruby personality may work extremely hard at something that they are enthusiastic about. Just be careful not to overheat in the July sun and get burned out or exhausted. There is a lot of forward momentum and uplifting energy when you are around your July-born friends.

Themes for July children:

- Very passionate within relationships
- Creative and innovative thinking
- Incredibly self-motivated and inspiring to others

August (Peridot)

August is the final month of summer. If you are a student, you are getting ready to go back to school. Often people take vacations to close out the summer before the rush of work begins again. This is a month of taking those final opportunities before starting in at focused efforts. Peridot is a stone that helps us make that transition. It is supportive in letting go of what we no longer need to make room for new growth and opportunities. It is difficult to start in on a new project if we are still involved in an old one or won't bring it to a close. Peridot also encourages not being attached to harmful and unhealthy emotions. Holding onto bitterness about the past prevents us from moving forward in our days, lives, and relationships.

Themes for August children:

- Releasing what is completed and welcoming new opportunities
- Creating balance in life by reducing multitasking
- Not letting negative emotions linger and control your actions

September (Sapphire)

In September, we are moving into the fall and the quieter, darker, and colder months. There is a new crispness in the air that causes us to snuggle into our coats, gathering our heat inward. This time also signals the start of learning for many schools and universities. Sapphire is the Stone of Wisdom and represents the balance of intellectual and inner knowledge. This stone encourages absorbing wisdom in all its forms from all different sources. It isn't limited to book or classroom learning, but also from tapping into the inner wisdom to see what the intuition wants you to learn as well. The deep blue is also a stone of communication and sapphire souls often desire to share their collective knowledge with others. This is a month and stone for teachers and students alike and all those driven by the love of learning.

Themes for September children:

- Having a thirst for knowledge
- Checking the external knowledge with the inner wisdom. Does it feel true to you?
- Teaching and sharing wisdom with others

October (Pink Tourmaline and Opal)

October is a time of harvest—of clearing out fields of the ripe crops and then sowing under to prepare to rest for the winter. This month we reap the benefits of our labors. What we have planted and nurtured in life will now provide fruit (or pumpkins). This ties deeply into karma and ensuring that the things we are nurturing are the ones we truly want to manifest in our lives. It is the trick-or-treat moment in life. Did we sow positivity and get the treat or negativity and get the trick? Pink Tourmaline and Opal work together to remind the October souls that compassion and heart-centered motivation will provide us and the world with amplified cycles of positivity and love. The October child has the potential to be a great beacon of light during the darkness of winter.

Themes for October children:

- Learning the consequences of our actions
- Knowing the effect we can have on the energy of the world
- Sharing optimism and compassion when times are dark

November (Citrine and Topaz)

The color of golden yellow is especially appropriate during the month of November because winter has settled in. We're done with the joy of "pumpkin spice season," and it's *cold*. This is a time when we want to be reminded of the sun and warmth. We need a little brightness to get us through the long winter. Both Citrine and Topaz are golden yellow stones that stimulate the solar plexus chakra and that chakra's associated element is *fire*. These are stones that both boost motivation, optimism, and confidence. They encourage us to shine brightly, see the beauty in life, and get out there to make something happen. For those born in November, these are qualities you'll be needing to develop and strengthen in your life. If you feel like you are already pretty connected to these qualities, then make the most of them. Take charge of your world and let those around you see you shine!

Themes for November children:

- Motivation and confidence

- Appreciation of the beauty in life

- Leadership and initiating change in the world

December (Turquoise, Blue Topaz, and Blue Zircon)

December is a time of quiet, solitude, hibernation, rest, and reflection. The year is coming to an end and many people spend time thinking about what they've done over the course of the year. This is a time for curling up on the couch under warm blankets and resting. Now, Tanzanite and Turquoise are blue gemstones, Zircon comes in blue as well, and all of these stones stimulate the throat chakra. The throat chakra is our seat of communication, authenticity, and wisdom. Blue is the color of getting to know yourself—of quiet, inner reflection, and accessing our own inner wisdom. This is perfect for winter's quiet depth when we're reflecting on the transition to the new year and what we want to do with the next cycle in our lives.

Themes for December children:

- Feeling centered after quiet and solitude

- Ease with the practice of inner reflection

- Skill at communication and sharing your authentic wisdom with the world

What Is Your Zodiac Sign?

Knowing which stones resonate with your zodiac sign will help strengthen your connection to that gemstone during practice. Gemstones are connected to a zodiac sign because the qualities it supports are also supportive of the energy of that zodiac personality. However, everyone can use any stone during this practice. Do not feel limited to just using stones connected to your sign. But since we tend to be drawn to elements, colors, and aspects of our astrology signs, using crystals with an energetic affiliation with our zodiac sign helps strengthen your energetic relationship with that stone.

Practices may feel like they work faster, are easier to absorb and understand, or are more intense with zodiac stones. Consider your birth sign below and see if you feel drawn to any of these gemstones. This may help you in choosing between the various gemstones for life situations.

Also, note that there are many, many gemstones per zodiac sign. This is because there is a vast array of gemstones and they are all connected to one or more signs. There is no gemstone that doesn't resonate with at least one zodiac sign. A few gemstones, like Clear Quartz and Moldavite, resonate with all zodiac signs. A gemstone may have energetic properties that support multiple zodiac personalities. You can explore the full selection in depth at my website, www.crystal-wisdom.com.

Here is a selection of the most common and accessible gemstones for each zodiac sign:

- Capricorn: December 22 - January 20 (Tiger's Eye, Black Tourmaline, Malachite, Fluorite)

- Aquarius: January 21 - February 18 (Garnet, Amber, Angelite, Hematite)

- Pisces: February 19 - March 19 (Amethyst, Blue Lace Agate, Gold Topaz, Fluorite)

- Aries: March 20 - April 19 (Apache Tear, Aventurine, Bloodstone, Aquamarine)

- Taurus: April 20 - May 20 (Carnelian, Red Jasper, Diamond, Rhodonite)

- Gemini: May 21 - June 20 (Emerald, Apatite, Celestite, Howlite)

- Cancer: June 21 - July 22 (Calcite, Moonstone, Opal, Tektite)

- Leo: July 23 - August 22 (Amber, Citrine, Jasper, Labradorite)

- Virgo: August 23 - September 22 (Amazonite, Snowflake Obsidian, Peridot, Dalmatian Stone)

- Libra: September 23 - October 22 (Ametrine, Iolite, Jade, Lepidolite)

- Scorpio: October 23 - November 21 (Charoite, Unakite, Turquoise, Malachite)

- Sagittarius: November 22 - December 21 (Lapis Lazuli, Herkimer Diamond, Obsidian, Sodalite)

What Is Your Life Path Number?

I have found that numerology can be a valuable asset in determining our life themes and how our personality types contribute to our successes and challenges in life. Understanding some of our personality's driving forces can help us work within our lives' flow rather than struggling. In this section, I'll show you how to find Crystal Wisdom with your Life Path Number. This is a concept in numerology that describes certain personality types based on the numeral of your birth date.

Numerology is a practice that stems from Pythagoras' studies of numbers and their relation to the natural world. Christine DeLorey describes the effect of numbers wonderfully: "Numbers are *natural* elements; major effects of space and time that enable us to measure and understand our world, and beyond it." The field of numerology states there is an energy and a meaning to all numbers and that tapping into the numerical value of aspects of our lives can provide great wisdom and guidance.

In this step, calculate your Life Path Number and refer to it in the descriptions below. I offer a gemstone that can help support and cultivate these personality traits in your life. To figure out your Life Path Number, you will take your numerical birthdate and condense it down to a *one-digit number*. If the birthdate is June 13, 1982, you would write it out as 6+13+1982. Add these together to get the number 2001. Then keep adding the numbers together until you reduce them to one digit: 2+0+0+1 equals 3. This birthdate indicates a Life Path of 3, the Creator. If you are a Creator type in your life but continue to pursue careers with little to no creativity, this can cause suffering and dissatisfaction. Maybe your current job can be improved by incorporating more creative aspects into it. Knowing your personality type—and the crystal that can support it—enables you to tap into a well of inner talent and strengths.

1 Life Path: The Leader (Sunstone – Personal Power)

The Leader is an innovative, creative driving force. They are charismatic and take the World by storm to influence its direction. The Sunstone helps people with creativity, confidence, leadership, and abundance. If you are on Life Path 1 and feeling a little uninspired, then wear Sunstone to give you a boost with your mission!

2 Life Path: The Peacemaker (Sodalite – Community)

The Peacemaker is a person who expresses the voice of cooperation, harmony, kindness, and universal vision. Sodalite is a stone that helps us own our True Voice and to use it to bring communities together. If you are on Life Path 2 and feel at a loss about your message, sit with Sodalite to allow the Highest Good to manifest through you.

3 Life Path: The Creator (Carnelian – The Artist's Stone)

The Creator is full of vision, life, artistry, and expression that they share with the World to make it brighter and more alive. Carnelian is an energetic stone that stimulates creative thinking and the ability to bring visions into reality. If you feel like you have Writer's Block, wear Carnelian to get the creative juices flowing again.

4 Life Path: The Organizer (Hematite – Stone of the Mind)

The Organizer can plan, build, and works with integrity and determination. The work gets done effectively and efficiently. Hematite grounds our mind into calm, structured thinking and planning. If you are on Life Path 4 and feeling at a loss for direction, sit with Hematite to focus your thoughts and work on the next step.

5 Life Path: The Adventurer (Malachite – Stone of Transformation)

The Adventurer is all about freedom, exploration, and pushing the boundaries of life! Malachite is an extremely protective stone that helps us during travel and significant transitions in life. If you are on Life Path 5 and about to start on your next adventure, make sure to carry a piece of Malachite with you.

6 Life Path: The Nurturer (Moonstone – Stone of Reflection)

The Nurturer is dedicated to providing comfort, beauty, and kindness to friends and family. Moonstone is the stone of Mother Moon and connects us with the Divine Feminine to provide a safe place for a family to grow. If you are on Life Path 6 and feeling a bit tired and strained, Moonstone reminds you to take care of yourself as well.

7 Life Path: The Truth Seeker (Amethyst – Spirituality and Wisdom)

The Truth Seeker is a person who is looking for the ultimate connection to Higher Self. They spend much time studying, meditating, and in Spiritual Practice. Amethyst helps to open our consciousness and connect us with great Universal Information. If you are on Life Path 7 and seeking Wisdom and Connection, meditating and listening with Amethyst will help you find Ultimate Peace.

8 Life Path: The Powerhouse (Citrine – Abundance and Prosperity)

The Powerhouse takes charge in the business world! They build, maintain, and make businesses and projects thrive. They attract opportunities to prosper! Citrine is the Master of all Abundance Stone, as it energizes, boosts confidence, enhances decisiveness, encourages wise business choices, and attracts abundance into your life. If you are on Life Path 8 and worried about a current or upcoming venture, wear Citrine to help you regain confidence.

9 Life Path: The Humanitarian (Rose Quartz – Unconditional Love)

The Humanitarian has a heart committed to helping others and inspiring love and generosity. Rose Quartz helps keep the heart chakra wide open to manifest the courage to give and receive love and support. If you are on Life Path 9 and having some difficulty being compassionate about a current person or situation, wear Rose Quartz to remind you of your Heart Center.

Throughout these chapters, you have identified a selection of life challenges or goals and assigned them gemstones to act as your support system. We will be developing easy, practical meditations for you to incorporate on a daily and as-needed basis. If your selection is more than six stones at this point, you may want to consider placing a few aside for later practices. I don't want this practice to become cumbersome or overwhelming in your life. Over time, you will expand your ability to work with more and more stones at a time. The gemstones that remain will help you initiate change in your life, improve your experiences during your days, and manifest new opportunities due to these changes.

CHAPTER 8

Buying Your Gemstones

Finding a Reputable Source

Now that you've identified the gemstones that will comprise your Guardian Gemstone team, the extra fun part starts—collecting them! If you don't already have these crystals in your collection, then you'll need to find and buy them. There are three primary ways to buy your gemstones: in a local brick-and-mortar store, an online store, or at a gemstone expo or convention.

I highly recommend trying a local store first. There is a considerable benefit to looking at and holding the crystals before you choose them, and you have someone available right there to answer your questions. Also, supporting local businesses is encouraged. In a gem store, you have direct access to the energy of the stones. Take your time, hold the stones, see which one feels the most comfortable. You can browse through the entire selection, look at each one, and see which one draws your attention the most. You are also able to judge the quality of the stones right there in the store. You will not be surprised or disappointed by what you bring home. What you see, and feel, is what you get.

You can also purchase gemstones online, which is an excellent source if you don't have access to a nearby store. There is also a wider variety of crystals available across the internet. However, this can be an overwhelming task as there are thousands of online gemstone sellers. How do you choose? First, use care and caution when selecting an online seller. You may not always receive what you expected from a picture. Sometimes the picture is an "example" of what you might receive, and what you get is absolutely not what you expected. It's also not easy to judge the size of a gemstone from a picture. It may not always be clear if a gemstone is natural, synthetic, or treated. If you find a reliable and trusted online seller, bookmark the site and use it regularly.

Don't worry—online shopping *can* be fun and reliable. Here are some tips for online buying. Try to choose a seller that will provide the specific gemstone in the picture. It's even better if there are multiple pictures of the gemstone at different angles. Have a ruler and scale available so you can see how large something actually is. If a size is listed, take a peek at the ruler and see if that is the size you'd like. If the crystal is listed by weight, then place one of your gemstones on a scale to get a better picture of how a 10-gram gemstone looks. If the stone's size is displayed by placing it next to a coin, get that same coin to get a better sense of the size comparison. In my early shopping days, I was disappointed many times by receiving a gemstone that I thought was a different size or quality. If the seller is offering a random gemstone from a larger selection, then you won't know ahead of time what the gemstone will look like when you receive it. I recommend that you make a small purchase from a potential seller, ensure that you are happy with what you receive and the shipping time, then make larger purchases in the future. It is very easy to spend hundreds of dollars on one purchase, and you don't want to be disappointed when the entire large purchase isn't what you expected.

Another point to consider is ethical sourcing. This can be an important factor for some gemstone buyers. Ethical gemstone sources make sure that their mining practices do not negatively affect the earth, that they don't take advantage of cheap or slave labor, and that employee working conditions are safe. Many mines that employ intentional ethical practices will clearly advertise this to their resellers. If ethical sourcing is an essential factor for you, make sure to ask your seller before you make your purchase. However, this will often mean that the gemstones are more expensive to compensate for the additional certification measures and the reseller's effort to provide ethically sourced stones. Does this mean that every mine that doesn't specifically advertise ethical practices is unsafe or unfair to its workers? Absolutely not. They may just not feel the need to make that a marketing standout.

Choosing the Specific Crystal to Add to Your Collection

Now that you have your list of gemstones to shop for and have found some places where you can comfortably purchase your gemstones, how do you determine precisely which Aventurine or Howlite gemstone to buy? There are so many options and it's going to involve tapping into your inner wisdom to lead you to the right style of stone. This will take practice but will become more comfortable as you buy more gemstones and figure out your personal preferences.

One of the most common questions I receive is, "Does the size of a gemstone affect the amount of energy it provides?" No, it does not. The size of the gemstone does not matter. What is of primary importance is how you feel about the stone. The more you are drawn to a particular piece, the stronger your relationship will be with it, and it will be more effective during practice. If you find yourself looking at a selection of stones and you feel drawn to pick up and hold the really small piece, then don't feel pressured to buy one that's larger. There are some general size guidelines. It's easier for meditation if the stone can fit comfortably in your palm. Very large carvings or rough specimens are not easy to sit with in meditation. They are great pieces for placing in a room to give the room the energy of the gemstone, but for these Crystal Wisdom practices, you'll want something easy to hold or wear.

"Should the crystal be rough or polished?" "Can I buy a tower, sphere, or carving rather than a tumbled stone?" "Can I wear a bracelet instead of getting a loose stone?" The answer to all of these questions is, "It is purely up to your personal preference." A rough stone does not emit more energy than a polished one. You can also choose to wear your entire crystal collection. A bracelet or pendant can be just as effective as a palm stone or crystal point. Really let your intuition, personal preference, and attraction be your guide here. If you'd like an entire collection of carved obelisks or spheres, then do that. If you prefer raw stone over polished, that is perfect for you. Buy what you *want*, and you will feel much more connected to your gemstones during daily and spontaneous practices.

When it comes to narrowing a selection down to one specific stone for you to buy and bring home, see what you are attracted to most. Does the mix of colors in one stone draw your eye? Maybe you like a darker shade of the gemstone. There could be a pattern in the stone that you really like or even the shape of the stone itself. Don't worry if you don't have the opportunity to choose the specific stone to buy. If you are purchasing online and will receive a random gem selected by the seller, the Crystal Wisdom practice will still work. You will be able to connect with the stone as you work with it more and more.

Treated and Synthetic Gemstones

One final topic about gemstone purchasing is how treated and synthetic gemstones affect the Crystal Wisdom practice. These gemstones have been altered or even created in a lab. Will they still be effective?

Two common ways a gemstone can be treated are by dying or heating. A dyed gemstone has been dipped in a color solution and the exterior is dyed another color. This often happens with Agates, Quartz, and Howlite. As we previously discussed, a gemstone's color provides a lot of power and connection to our inner voice. We are attracted to a particular color for a reason. However, with dyed stones, this color is only skin deep. It doesn't penetrate the entire stone. The stone still holds the supportive benefits and properties of its original color—just like painting your fingernail doesn't actually alter the color of the nail itself, only the outside. My guidance is, if you find yourself attracted to a gemstone that is clearly dyed pink, then pink is a signal color for you, but you should probably explore genuine, natural pink stones instead. I do not use dyed gemstones in my meditation practices.

You can identify dyed gemstones in a few ways. The first is just knowing which gem colors are found in nature and which are not.

This takes time and experience with gemstones. If you are buying online, look in the listing for keywords like dyed, treated, or colored. The final way, if you received a stone that you suspect is dyed, is to perform an acetone test. Dip a Q-tip in acetone or fingernail polish remover and rub the Q-tip on the stone vigorously for a minute. If the color comes off onto the Q-tip, it has been dyed.

Heat-treated gemstones also have had their color changed. Many gemstones will change color when heated to a certain temperature. Unlike with dyed gemstones, heating will change the color all the way through a stone. It is for this reason that I *do* still use heat-treated gemstones in my Crystal Wisdom practice. The most widely debated heat-treated gemstone is Citrine, or rather, heat-treated Amethyst. When Amethyst is heated, it will turn a golden color. This is often sold as Citrine. Natural, untreated Citrine is scarce and is very expensive. It also has a lighter and smokier yellow tone. It is easy to identify heat-treated from natural when you see them side-by-side. I still work with heat-treated Citrine because its golden yellow color is an effective stimulator of the solar plexus chakra and the qualities that it supports. However, the energy it evokes is different than natural Citrine, which is cleaner and lighter. Red Tiger's Eye results from heating Gold Tiger's Eye. I have tumbled and polished Red Tiger's Eye and I can confirm that the stone is red all the way through. I find this gemstone effective at evoking the qualities of the root and sacral chakra. It's a powerful stone that I highly recommend. Other commonly heat-treated stones are Aquamarine, Topaz, Prasiolite, and Ametrine.

Aqua Aura crystals are another version of a treated gemstone. They are genuine quartz crystals fused with metals like gold, platinum, titanium, nickel, silver, and more. The quartz crystal points are created in a vacuum chamber with metal vapors. During the vacuum environment, the metal vapors are bonded to the exterior of the crystal. Different metals will produce different colors. These make beautiful pieces. I have worked with Aqua Aura and I do feel they have their own distinct and unique energies. The combination of metal fused with the crystal creates an energy that can clearly be sensed during meditation and practice. They all have their unique supportive benefits. There are at least 30 different types and are worth exploring for your Crystal Wisdom practice.

Synthetic stones are a completely different story. These gemstones were man-made in a lab. Synthetics never grew within the pressure and heat of the earth itself and do not connect with the energy and power inherent in earth-born gemstones. I do not use synthetic gemstones in my Crystal Wisdom practice because the energy does not feel any different than regular window glass. Synthetic stones still can be beautiful and make gorgeous jewelry or display pieces. Still, we are harnessing the natural, supportive energy that comes from being created within the earth itself for the Crystal Wisdom practice.

When you are shopping for gemstones, it is good to be aware of which stones can possibly be man-made or not. Companies often make synthetic gemstones because the natural form is expensive and scarce and it is cost-effective to make a less expensive version. If a gemstone is readily available and inexpensive, like Amethyst or Obsidian, for example, there isn't likely to be someone making synthetic versions. When you are shopping, look for keywords like synthetic, lab-grown, created, or man-made. Some common stones that are often sold as "gemstones" that are not: Goldstone (all colors), Opalite, Gaia Stone, Helenite, Cubic Zirconia, any Obsidian that does not have a base color of black (Red Obsidian, Blue Obsidian, etc.), and Andara Crystals.

The topic of Andara Crystals is highly debated. These "crystals" can sell for upwards of $10,000. The fields of geology and gemology do not recognize this as a genuine gemstone. These are not listed in any gemstone book or scientific mineral database. It has often been stated that Andara Crystals are leftover slag from glass factories. The purpose of this section is not to debate the authenticity of Andaras but to advise that you should be very cautious of buying anything for thousands of dollars that *could be* just glass.

For the final note in this section, I want to highlight some commonly fakes gemstones. Take a closer look when buying these gemstones to make sure you are purchasing natural, genuine pieces. Malachite, Rhodochrosite, and Larimar synthetic stones can be made from glass. Bottle green glass is often sold as Moldavite. Be especially skeptical of Moldavite that is faceted or beads. Howlite is often dyed blue and sold as Turquoise. Any semiprecious stone can be synthesized now, including Diamond, Ruby, Sapphire, Amethyst, Topaz, and Emerald. Opal synthetics are quite common on the market, while Aventurine and Chrysoprase are often sold as Jade.

I don't mean to frighten you about the potential for fraud when buying crystals and gemstones, but I don't want you to be disappointed or waste money either. Just look for a few keywords when buying: treated, dyed, colored, heated, created, lab-grown, synthetic, glass, and man-made. When buying in a store, if you are in doubt, ask your seller. Are you ready to go shopping?? Let's do it!

CHAPTER 9

Preparing Your Gemstones for Practice

Caring for Your Guardian Gemstones

You now have your set of Guardian Gemstones! Congratulations! Now that you've brought them home or received them in the mail, it is crucial to start a regular practice of caring for your gemstones. This is where you will begin to form a relationship with these gemstones. They will be there to help unlock your inner truth, support you when you need comfort, help you figure out better ways to react to life situations, and help to initiate change in your life. These are sacred tools, and they should be cared for and treated as important and cherished.

How you treat your gemstones will reflect how you treat yourself and your practice.

In Buddhist practice, the Dharma texts are sacred. They are not to be placed on the floor, near your feet, or stepped over. If this does happen, the student would touch the text to the crown of their head as a sign of respect and honor. This reinforces the importance that the wisdom texts have in the students' transformational journeys.

As you read through this section, you may want to write your preferences and ideas for your caring routine in your journal. How would you prefer to cleanse, charge, activate, and store your gems? How often will you perform these? Where in your home or yard will this take place? Then you can develop a regular Guardian Gemstone care plan in the final section of this chapter.

Cleansing Your Guardian Gemstones

After you receive new gemstones and before you meditate with them, you should perform a cleansing of your gemstones. You will also cleanse them regularly to clear away any accumulated energy within the crystals. It is important to perform a regular cleansing because gemstones do absorb the energy they are surrounded by. As a certain mood or energy can build up in a room, the same will happen with crystals. A room with frequent arguments and negativity will start to feel heavy and dark even to those who have just entered the room for the first time. A home that is the center of frequent parties and celebrations might take on a lighter and more festive mood. This is the same with gemstones. If you have received a brand-new stone, you'll want to clear away previous owners' energy or the store it was waiting in. If you are going to use stones in your practice that you've already owned but haven't cleansed recently, it is a good idea to give them a nice, refreshing cleanse.

There are many ways to cleanse gemstones, so the methods you choose are purely up to your personal preference. Write down some of the ideas that stand out to you while you read. Some of the most common means of cleansing are water, earth, air, other gemstones, and Reiki.

Cleansing gemstones with water is one of the easiest ways to clean your gemstones. Clean, fresh water can eliminate any stagnant energy that has accumulated. The water can even be tap water; however, it is better if the water is filtered. You can run the gemstones under the faucet. This will wash the stale energy down the drain and lay them on a soft towel to dry. Sea or river water is also a strong water cleanser. Just make sure the body of water you use has some flow and is not stagnant.

I really enjoy setting my gemstones out during the rain. I have a special bowl that I place any gemstones in need of a little freshening in the bowl. When it starts to rain outside, I take the bowl to a specific place I have chosen and let the stones receive the rain's deep cleansing energy. A storm is even better as the energy is strong and lightning deepens the process. Some of my clients save jars of rainwater to use for regular gemstone cleaning between rains. Place some designated jars out in the rain to collect as much as you can. When the rain is over, close up the jar and set it in a window so the sun will keep it clean and charged. Many are concerned about water-sensitive stones and I will discuss that topic in Chapter 14, *"Common Crystal Questions"*.

Earth is a powerful cleanser of crystals. If you don't connect with the water element, or it just doesn't rain enough where you live, you can set your gemstones directly on the earth. Any excess and accumulated energies will be absorbed back into the earth. If you have a yard, this is easier. Identify a place in the yard that will serve as your cleansing area. It should be in the shade or done at night so that sun-sensitive stones will not fade. You will learn more about which stones are sensitive to sunlight in the common questions section of Chapter 14. Then lay your crystals directly on the earth. It doesn't have to be bare soil. The gemstones can rest on the grass as that is also an extension of the earth. Let the crystals rest there for several hours or overnight to allow them to release this extra energy down into the ground.

If you do not have a yard, then you can make a special place in your home for the same purpose. Plant pots are a great container for this practice. Fill a deep bowl or planter with soil and dirt. Keep this in a low traffic area in your house and you can perform the cleansing practice with your special altar of earth. If you have pets, you may want to keep this higher as they tend to dig in the dirt. I've learned from experience!

Incense can also be used to cleanse gemstones. This method is a combination of the power of Fire and Air elements. You can burn sage, palo santo, or your favorite sacred incense. Sage is often used to perform a deep cleansing of energies from objects, people, and spaces. It will eliminate all accumulated energies and leave the space at a fresh starting point. This is excellent for brand-new gemstones. Palo Santo is often used to dissolve only accumulated *negative* energy but allows the accumulated positive and sacred energies to remain. This is appropriate for cleansing a room or crystal that has been used in sacred practice for some time, thus building up the positive energy of the practice and only needing freshening up. To perform the cleansing, hold a crystal and move it slowly through the smoke. This will enable the accumulated negative or stale energy to drift away with the smoke.

Another effective way to cleanse gemstones, especially sun and water-sensitive ones, is to use other gemstones for the cleansing process. Selenite, White Calcite, Carnelian, Kyanite, and Citrine are all-powerful stones that will transmute the energy of other gemstones. I have a Selenite plate that I use for this purpose. I place the gemstones that need cleansing on the plate for several hours and any stale, stagnant, or excess energy will be transmuted and released from the crystals. You can also keep one of these cleansing gems in your sacred box of Guardians and it will keep them always fresh and ready for use.

The final method I enjoy is cleansing crystals using Reiki energy. If you are a Reiki practitioner or know one who can perform this for you, then you can perform Reiki on your gemstones to clean them. This is a practice that only requires the basic Reiki Level 1 training and is especially useful because you can cleanse your gemstones at any time in just a few minutes. The Reiki practitioner would sit with the stones cupped between the palms of their hands and allow the Reiki to flow into the gemstones for a few minutes. This is all it takes to perform a complete gemstone cleansing. You can explore Reiki certification opportunities at my website, www.crystal-wisdom.com/online-courses.

Finally, how often should you cleanse your gemstones? At a minimum, you should have a regular schedule in which you perform a routine cleansing. Once a month is a good starting point. Sometimes gemstones need to be cleared between maintenance sessions, so it's good to have a plan ready for spontaneous cleansings. If you start to feel that it's harder to connect with your gemstone, it doesn't seem to be as effective, and just feels dull when you pick it up, it is probably in need of a good washing and charging.

Charging Your Guardian Gemstones

Once your gemstones have been cleansed, then you'll want to charge them up with positive energy to help fuel your Crystal Wisdom practices. I consider this practice like a morning routine. I might start with a warm shower, which helps me feel clean and awake, but now I need breakfast to provide energy for the day. Common ways of charging crystals are with moon, sun, crystal, and Reiki energies.

Leaving your sacred gemstones out in the moonlight can fill them with powerful moon energy. Consider what a potent effect the moon has on the earth and our bodies. The moon influences the tides of the ocean and menstrual cycles. The moon's energy will provide strong and positive energy to aid our use of crystals during our practices. In fact, preparing and setting your gemstones out during the full or new moon can become very special and sacred ritual evenings in your personal practice. You can charge gems with moonlight on any night; it doesn't matter how much moonlight we can perceive, it will still charge the stones.

For a moon-charging practice, you'll want to find a special plate to act as your little altar. I cover mine with a special cloth so the crystals are not placed directly on a hard plate. Then place your Guardian Gemstones on the plate. You can set the gem altar in a windowsill or directly outside. This just depends on how secure you feel leaving your gems outside. Let it soak in the moon energy overnight and they will be ready for use in the morning.

The sun can also be a powerful gemstone-charging source. The uplifting, warming energy of the sun can provide powerful fuel for our Crystal Wisdom practice. Do be aware that some gemstones are sun-sensitive (see Chapter 14 for more on this) and so you can perform the same ritual as the moon-charging practice, but only leave the gemstones out in the sun for about five minutes. Don't worry, the sun is strong and vibrant and so it will work quickly.

You can also charge your gemstones by placing them on or near a Clear Quartz crystal or cluster. Clear Quartz is the Stone of Amplification and will boost the energy and support of the gemstones that are near it. You can also keep Clear Quartz in the place where you decide to store your gemstones for continual charging energy.

Finally, Reiki is also a potent energy to charge your gemstones. Just as with cleansing your gemstones with Reiki, this is a quick and easy practice. It only takes a few minutes. Often, Reiki practitioners perform cleansing and charging one right after the other. They take a few minutes to cleanse, then right after, a few minutes to charge. It is a quick and effective practice you can perform at any time.

Activating Your Guardian Gemstones (Setting the Intention)

Now that your gemstones are cleansed and charged, the most important step in the preparation process begins: setting the intention for the gemstone. In the crystal-healing world, this is often called activating your crystals. This activation process is saying, "Now let's begin our work." However, work can't begin until we set a very clear and intentional purpose for each gemstone. This only needs to be done once, but it is a vital step. If you don't have a specific purpose for the Guardian Gemstone, you won't know when to use it and you won't start seeing results.

This activating process should be completed for each Guardian Gemstone, but these can all be done in one session, one after another. To prepare for the intention-setting meditation, sit down with your journal or Guardian Gemstone worksheet. Review the life situations you had identified with each gemstone. On another sheet of paper, write the name of the gemstone and a request to assist you with that life situation. This is its intention.

For example, if I chose Rhodonite to help me handle tensions and disagreements with family members, then I would write, "Rhodonite, please help me have a healthy relationship with this person even though we disagree." Or, if I chose Howlite to help me reduce feelings of stress and anxiety, I might write, "Howlite, please help me to release stress and anxiety whenever it strikes." This is a simple practice, but it is the very seed you are planting to start manifesting positive change in your life.

Next, find a quiet place to sit with your gemstones. Have your list of gemstone intentions nearby. If you have a bell, chime, or sound bowl, it will be extra helpful during this practice. Pick up each gemstone and hold it in your dominant hand. Then read your request out loud. Take a minute to allow this intention and request to settle into the gemstone. You are imbuing it with the power to help you make change and improvement in your life. Then I recommend sealing the intention request with the sound of a bell. Your crystals are now ready for your daily and spontaneous practices, which you'll learn about in the next chapters.

Storing Your Guardian Gemstones

How you store your gemstones in between use is a vital part of your sacred gemstone care plan. There are many ways you can store your crystals, but make sure that the space is easily accessible when you need them. It will be important to be able to pick one up when you feel that you need it and sit for your spontaneous practice. You may want to have a storage place for home and one that is portable for taking out into the world. Here are some suggestions. You can use one or multiple, and it should be up to your personal preference.

Having a display shelf for your gemstones is a popular method. This could be on a small altar, a bookshelf, fireplace mantle, or a shadow box. I have my team of Writing Gemstones on my desk on a special lotus plate so I can look at and pick up my crystals when I need support while writing this book. My Writing Gemstones are a secondary team of Guardian Gemstones explicitly created for this project. It is nice to see your team whenever you pass by and be reminded of your life-supporting goals. I would avoid displaying gemstones on a windowsill. While they are beautiful in the sunlight, it could cause sun-sensitive gemstones to fade. (I'll discuss sun-sensitive gemstones in more detail in Chapter 14.)

Special boxes are also a great place to store your gemstones and are portable as well. I have a few boxes that I have picked out just for my gems. Buying a sacred box can be a special event. You can get a pretty box, line the bottom with a soft cloth or cushion, and place your gemstones inside. Make sure there is enough room for them all to fit in with some space in between. You can add a cleansing and/or charging crystal in with your team if you wish. This benefit of a box is that it can hold in all that sacred energy and you can carry it between rooms to have nearby when needed.

Decorative bags are useful for bringing gemstones with you when you head out into the world. If you have gemstones that will help you at work, in social situations, or to protect you from the energy of others, having the crystals in a bag in your purse, pocket, or car will ensure they are available when you need them. I have a piece of Blue Calcite in my purse to help when I'm out shopping. The Blue Calcite protects empathic people from absorbing the emotions and energies of others. I can hold Blue Calcite to help me strengthen my personal energy field and not accumulate others' energies.

You can plan multiple ways to store your crystals in between use. I use all three of these methods. The key with storage is to have a sacred space for your gemstones to rest at home or on the go so that they don't get knocked about in daily life. This will enable you to reflect on the importance they hold in your life, along with your sacred intentions, and to have them accessible for use when you need them. If you are in a difficult situation but forgot to bring your gemstone with you, then you won't be able to use your practice to support you.

Creating Your Gemstone Care Plan

Now that you know the importance of caring for your gemstones, it's time for you to think about and write down your Gemstone Care Plan. This will ensure a comfortable and regular flow for your caretaking ritual. Here are some questions to ask yourself as you prepare your plan:

Cleansing:

- What method(s) would you like to use to clean your gemstones?

- What supplies do you need to get to start this method?

- Where will you perform this practice?

- How often will you cleanse your stones?

Charging:

- What method(s) would you like to use to charge your gemstones?

- What supplies do you need to get to start this method?

- Where will you perform this practice?

- How often will you charge your stones?

Activating: This usually only takes place with new gemstones or when changing the intention of a stone.

- Where will you perform your intention-setting practice?

- What supplies do you need to get to begin?

Storing:

- What method(s) would you like to use to store your gemstones?

- Where will you most often need to access your gemstones?

- What supplies do you need to get to start this method?

PART II

Your Crystal Wisdom Practice

Cultivating Your Own

Crystal Wisdom Practice

CHAPTER 10

How to Meditate with Gemstones

Now that you've selected your Guardian Gemstones and know how to care for them, let's get down to the core of how to work with them in practice. We'll start by setting the scene, preparing your space, learning some basics about meditation, and understanding how the gemstone energy and support may feel to you. This information will provide the foundation for the unique practices you'll design in the next chapter. You will be performing two types of Crystal Wisdom practices: daily and spontaneous. The daily practices will allow you to sit each day with a specific stone and life situation, reflect on how you feel about it, how it may have changed over time, and then journal about your reflections afterward. Spontaneous practices will happen in the moment when you need them. Feeling some overwhelming stress right now? Grab your Lepidolite and sit to observe how it makes you feel and how you can best respond to it. That's a vital component of a flowing and flexible, spontaneous practice.

Let's begin. How do you prepare for your meditation sessions?

Creating Your Meditation Space

It's important to have a regular space to sit and perform your daily practice in order to cultivate a regular routine and to help you settle quickly into the Crystal Wisdom reflection process. This is a space that you will carve out from the rest of your daily life and reserve for sitting in quiet. The more often you meditate, the stronger and more familiar your meditation space's energy will become, and you'll be able to settle into your inner wisdom space quickly.

Your Crystal Wisdom daily practice should occur in a quiet space in your home that won't be getting much traffic from the rest of your household members. You want to be able to sit and focus on your internal experience, the feeling of the gemstone energy, and how you feel about the life situation you are addressing with the crystal. It is difficult to do this with lots of noise and distractions. You do not need to set aside an entire room for your practice, just a small space in a room where you can close the door and have some solitude.

You'll need a seat for your sessions. This could be a meditation cushion (often called a zafu or zabuton) on the floor. If sitting cross-legged on a cushion is uncomfortable, you can also sit in a chair. Whichever chair you select should be comfortable but not so soft that you drift off to sleep. This chair should be reserved just for this practice. Pulling in a dinner chair every day for your practice will disrupt the energy of the space and be an extra bit of work you need to do before practice, therefore, making the process a little cumbersome. You want to be able to have a regular, set space that you can sit in at a moment's notice.

You may also want to set up relaxing and spiritual objects in your meditation space. Having a small table nearby to place a candle, incense, journal, bell, gemstones, or any critical spiritual items will mark this space as sacred. Setting the scene like this, and creating a designated meditation space, will encourage and reinforce your practice and enable you to tap into the gemstone energy and your inner wisdom easily and quickly. This intentional space marks your practice as special, sacred, and devoted to your own personal growth and development.

There will be times when you perform your spontaneous practices wherever you happen to be, which is entirely acceptable. I encourage you to bring your practices into your daily life. It expands your reflection and healing process out from one small meditation space to incorporating it wherever you are. Most of my gemstone sessions happen right in the middle of the bustle of life. If I feel scattered and disorganized while working, I'll sit in my workspace with some Fluorite to help me focus and organize my thoughts. If I need some patience while teaching my kids, I will sit with Howlite right there in the learning room and invite patience in with us. If I recognize the life situation I have chosen, I often just get my stone, sit down right where I am, and reflect on how that situation makes me feel and how I can best address it. This is how you truly start incorporating Crystal Wisdom into your everyday life.

Learning the Meditation Posture

For your daily practice, you'll want to sit in a comfortable position that will allow you to be alert and pay attention to the wisdom rising within. Proper posture will allow you to focus less on any physical discomforts and more on how your body, heart, and mind are reacting to your life situation. It's hard to notice the soft, subtle voice of your inner wisdom when your sitting position is causing your back to ache.

Whether you're on a cushion or a chair, sit up straight but not stiff like a toy soldier. Imagine a string is running from your tailbone, up your spine, and out the top of your head. Then you gently pull the string up and straighten yourself. There should be some looseness but not hunching over. Bring your shoulders back just a touch. This will help open up the heart space and allow you to breathe easier. Tuck your chin down so your gaze rests on the floor in front of you rather than straight ahead. This also allows for greater airflow into your lungs. Check that your tongue is relaxed in your mouth and not stuck to the roof of your mouth.

You should be able to inhale through your nose and out your mouth easily. You can rest your hands lightly on your lap, palms up or down. I recommend putting your palms down if you feel you need centering and grounding. Palms up is excellent if you want more energy or to be more alert. You will have a gemstone in one hand but your closed hand with the gem can still be positioned either up or down. In this position, you should be able to breathe fully and efficiently. Your energy will be able to flow unimpeded throughout your body.

If you have chosen to sit on a cushion, make sure that your sitting bones are evenly planted on the cushion so that you're not leaning right or left but solidly in the center. This provides secure grounding and connection to the earth during this practice. If your hips or knees tend to ache after a few minutes, you may want to have additional supports available to place under your outer thighs to alleviate the pressure. These could be small pillows or even folded towels.

For sitting in a chair, make sure that you can place the soles of your feet flat against the floor. This firm contact to the ground is your source of grounding and centering during this practice. Crossed legs or ankles will not allow the energy to flow evenly and openly through your body.

If you are not used to sitting in meditation, it may take a few weeks to get accustomed to this posture. That is completely normal. Be gentle with yourself and your process of learning. It will start to feel more natural the more you practice. It is okay to move and adjust your position during your meditations. You are not required to be an unmoving statue.

Sitting with Your Gemstones

Now that you know how to sit, there is some guidance that is specific to meditating with gemstones. You will want to sit with a stone that can be easily held in your hand. We covered this in a previous chapter, but it's relevant to repeat it here. Trying to hold a really large stone during meditation will be uncomfortable and distracting.

One question I often receive is, "Which hand should hold the stone?" The answer will depend on your intention and how you prefer the energy to flow. Most often, because you will want to be receiving the gemstone's energy, you will hold it in your non-dominant hand. This is the hand you *do not write with*. It is referred to as the receiving hand. If your intention is to send energy out, such as healing energy, love, or forgiveness to someone, then you will hold the crystal in your dominant hand, the hand you write with. This is called the sending hand. If you are ambidextrous, you should designate one hand for receiving, the other for sending, and *be consistent* with that in practice.

It is recommended that when sitting for daily practice, you make skin contact with the stone. This helps to strengthen your connection to the stone and its energy. You will be able to feel its surface texture, the weight in your hand, and feel it warm to your touch. However, if you are working with a gemstone in a pendant and the frame prevents you from making strong contact with the stone, that is perfectly fine. The practice will still work.

If you happen to drop your gemstone on the floor, then pick it up and touch it to the crown of your head. This is an act of honoring and showing respect and reverence for your sacred tools.

How Long Will It Take to Develop the Gemstone Connection?

This is the most common question I am asked about working with gemstone energy. The honest answer is, "It will depend." Over time, and with consistent practice, you will start to feel its effects more and more quickly. If you are brand-new to working with gemstones, it will take longer to recognize when you notice the crystal's support. But each time you sit with your gemstone, hold it in your hand, open up to explore that aspect of your life, the quicker it will be to tap into that space each and every day. When your relationship is firmly developed with a crystal, you will be able to pick it up and feel yourself opening to and receive its benefits almost immediately.

How does this feel? It also depends on what part of your life you are working on. For example, I often use Amazonite to clear my active and busy mind at the end of the day. Before I go to bed, I pick up the Amazonite, close my eyes and breathe, then ask myself to release the thoughts my mind is so attached to. When I first started this practice, it took five to ten minutes for me to release and calm my mind for sleep. Now when I do this, I can noticeably feel the swirling and insistent thoughts dissolving from my mind within seconds. It's a rapid process. If you are working on relieving stress, it could take many minutes to finally feel the stress, tension, and anxiety start to melt away. Still, with practice, you'll eventually feel this melting and dissolving happen very quickly. Sometimes it's more subtle, like when encouraging authenticity with Sodalite. The more you sit with the intention of living in a more authentic way, the easier it is to feel comfortable being yourself and expressing your truth.

The key is, the more you practice, the faster you will open up to and experience the support of the gemstone. The more you sit with the gemstone *and* your specific life-changing intention, the more you will invite change into your life. The more you will discover about yourself and the way you desire to live this life. That is the alchemy of Crystal Wisdom. Keep up the daily practices, and most importantly, recognize when you need a spontaneous practice and sit with it in the moment as soon as you can. It is this focused intention of sitting with a situation, in the moment, and looking at how you experience it that will naturally transition you into living a more engaged, fulfilling, and intentional life.

CHAPTER 11

Building Your Daily Practice

By this point, you should have your team of Guardian Gemstones, your journal, and your meditation space set up so that we can delve into your Crystal Wisdom practice. The daily practice is a foundational element of the Crystal Wisdom process that will slowly and steadily aid in creating lasting change. The spontaneous practices will support you "in the heat of the moment." After this chapter, you'll have the tools and plan to enable you to sit each day and cultivate the wisdom within. This practice is intended to be performed each day, spending a few minutes examining challenging areas of your life or qualities you want to develop and expand. This intentional time will allow you to uncover insight into how you can work with the life situation rather than avoid it or struggle against it. This valuable time will help you make a positive change in your life.

The Daily Practice

Designate a time each day when you can sit without being interrupted. This could be before everyone else in your house wakes up, during a mid-day break, or in the evening when you're winding down. It is entirely up to your personal preference. If you're unsure, you may want to try various times to see if you feel more comfortable or receptive at a particular time of day. Try to set aside approximately 20 minutes for this practice—10 minutes to reflect with your gemstone and 10 minutes to journal.

Before you begin, decide which gemstone and life situation you'd like to sit with. While you're new to this practice, I recommend focusing on just one per day and working through them in a rotation day after day. If you've chosen four gemstones, for example, then you'd work with just one for each day, then start over with the first one after the four days are complete. As you become more familiar with the practice, you can sit and intuitively decide which gemstone wants to speak to you. In the beginning, I recommend working with a regular schedule so you can get to know them each equally.

I recommend having a routine or ritual to set up or begin your practice. This could be lighting incense or a candle, ringing a bell, saying a short prayer to your angels or spirit guides, or chanting some mantras. This is something to signal the beginning of your practice.

1. Pick up the stone and place it in the receiving or sending hand, depending on your life challenge.

2. Close your eyes and focus on the feeling of breathing. This will draw your attention away from external concerns and into your body, where you will tap into the Crystal Wisdom. Just breathe for about a minute or 10 slow breaths.

3. Bring your attention to the gemstone in your hand. Notice how it feels in your hand, the weight, the shape, the texture. Turn it about in your hand and in your mind; send it a

message of thanks. "Thank you for assisting me today with (fill in the blank here)."

4. Bring to mind the life situation you want support with.

5. Notice what emotions this situation brings with it.

6. Where do you feel these emotions in your body? This is important. We know we're feeling emotion because of the physical sensations that arise when we experience it. It's important to be able to locate this in the body.

7. How strong is the emotion? Is it mild, significant, or somewhere in the middle?

8. Ask your Inner Guide, "Please tell me more about the source of my challenge." This question is intended to provide more insight into what might be contributing to your struggle, fear, hesitation, or blocks. Allow several minutes for this wisdom to arise.

9. Ask your Inner Guide, "What do I need to improve this situation?" Allow several minutes for this wisdom to arise. Do not be discouraged if the message is hard to notice at first—it will get clearer with practice.

10. Thank your Inner Guide and your Guardian Gemstone for its guidance and then take a few more slow, deep breaths.

11. When you feel ready, open your eyes.

12. Take a few minutes to write down what you experienced during the meditation and the wisdom you received. You can refer to the sample daily practice journal entries at the end of the chapter for reference.

At this stage in your work with Crystal Wisdom, you will find that journaling is a vital aspect of this process of transformation. Change may not happen overnight, but as you go back and review your journal entries, you will start to notice the changes in the way you are feeling and responding to these challenges. I'll provide a journaling example at the end of this chapter, straight from my own journal, to serve as a guide for your own entries and to highlight the changes over time.

Hearing Your Inner Wisdom

This meditation practice asks you to listen for the wisdom of your Inner Guide, but what does that mean? How do I know I'm hearing the wisdom from my Inner Guide and not just making it up in my brain? This is a skill that becomes easier and more natural over time. There is a difference in how it feels when we think or figure something out versus allowing the message to arise from our spirit center.

To experiment, sit in a quiet place and think about how to make scrambled eggs. Think about what you need and how you would do the task. Where do you notice these thoughts? For me, it is in the front part of my head, but it could be different for you. There is a strong and direct feeling when "thinking" thoughts. You may even feel like your mind is working or furrow your brow a bit.

Then try to release your thinking brain from work for a few minutes. Take a few slow breaths to exhale away mind thought. Just like releasing a muscle that has been working or straining, imagine your brain is relaxing. Then ask the question, "What do I need most today?" Resist the urge to think about it or "figure it out." You may have to ask again if nothing arises. Then see what messages come to you. My inner wisdom messages feel like light whispers of words, images, emotions, or sensations drifting up from my heart and throat area. Again, this may be different for you and that's completely natural. The key is to practice this until you get a good sense of how "thought" versus "intuition" feels to you.

It's also important to know that your Inner Guide will never sound mean or critical of you. It is the loving heart center of you. It will be honest and truthful to you, but it will be kind in doing so. If you hear a mean voice, that is the voice of the Inner *Critic*. When critical or judging messages arise for you, take a deep inhale and exhale those critical thoughts away. They are not supportive or helpful in this process.

Cultivating Honesty and Authenticity

There are two more aspects to this practice that are important. You will not be able to initiate change if you don't welcome these into your reflections. These two aspects are honesty and authenticity, combined with a willingness to look at the dark parts. These are challenging but will fuel and accelerate your results if you embrace them.

Your Inner Guide is a dear friend that has your very best interests at heart. It offers truth, honesty, and an opportunity to live your life in a genuinely authentic way. But this friend is not going to lie to you. It is capable of letting you see the hard truths you may be avoiding or denying. In these sessions, it is okay to be honest with yourself, your journal, and your Inner Guide. Recognizing and acknowledging the truth about a situation will enable us to stop our suffering and struggle. As the saying goes, *The truth will set you free.*

Maybe the answer you receive is not what you wanted to hear. Write it down in your journal, let it sit with you during the day, and see how you feel about it during the next meditation with that situation. You don't have to make any immediate decisions or changes, but you should consider the messages your Inner Guide provides.

Looking into the Dark

This practice takes some courage and willingness to look into the shadows of ourselves. This may seem scary or overwhelming at first, but I assure you that your Inner Guide and Guardian Gemstones will support you in your exploration. To heal, you'll need to be able to sit with those wounds, fears, and regrets to be able to free yourself from the chains they are binding you with in life. The lotus flower is used as a symbol of enlightenment. It is a beautiful flower that grows up out of the mud and muck of the water. Through the difficulties and pain in life, there is growth and transformation. There is a window of light on the other side of the dark room.

Sitting with these tender and sensitive situations takes self-compassion and courage. These you have within you. The Guardian Gemstones will support your process. If there are tears or anger, let them flow. Take shorter practice sessions if needed and continue to journal. If you know that you will be working with a part of your life or past that may be especially painful, make sure to have a support system to help you. Have friends, family, and maybe a therapist available to reach out to when needed.

Interpreting Gemstone Sensations

You may notice during your meditations that you feel certain physical and energetic sensations or receive visual imagery. These are all part of the wisdom messages that will arise within you. I am often asked what a particular sensation means, and my answer is, "It depends." This may seem like a vague or frustrating answer, but it really does mean that the message is for *you* to decipher. It is not for someone else to tell you what it means to your heart and life.

I recommend including these sensations in your journal to see if the sensations repeat or change over time. You may start to ask yourself, "What does this sensation mean to me?" You could ask it directly during your meditation practice, such as, "Tell me more about the tingling sensation in my right arm." Allow your inner wisdom to provide you with the answers.

For example, Janelle described an experience to me. She had a regular practice with Rose Quartz. She would sit with it in her receiving hand, but she kept feeling a weight and heaviness in her opposite arm during multiple meditations. She asked me what this could mean, and I asked in return, "What does it seem like it means to you?" She sat with that for a day and responded the next day with this answer: "It says to me that my original intention is to be receiving more love, but my Inner Guide says that to receive love, I need to start sending it out." Janelle changed her practice to sit with it in her sending hand and the heavy sensations ceased. She felt lighter and much more optimistic after her sessions.

My husband got some great news about a project result at work that was causing him some anxiety. He still couldn't relax even after he got this good result. He asked me, "I should feel relieved, and I am, but I also have this huge knot in my center that just won't go away. Why is that?" And of course, I asked him as well, "What do *you* think it means?" He paused for a minute, considering the sensation in his body, and slowly said, "I think it's because I still doubt and I'm waiting for the other shoe to drop. For some unexpected disappointment to ruin this."

This kind of self-awareness is available when we slow down and pause to listen to our inner wisdom. Of course, it's up to each of us how deeply we want to explore these revelations. Your body will send you messages, and you do hold the answers within. This practice is about listening with more than our minds: It's about listening and hearing with our intuition, heart, and bodies. The crystal helps us to tune into a particular frequency of our life and listen more carefully there.

Journal Entries from a Sample Daily Practice

Here are some entries from my own personal journal to serve as a guide for your own journaling process in your Crystal Wisdom practice, but yours don't have to look exactly like this. There is flexibility and creativity welcome in this practice. If you'd like to draw, add relevant inspirational quotes, or anything that relates to that situation, feel free to add it as well.

In this first entry, I am exploring my initial session with my gemstone. This records a "starting place" of my self-exploration with this life situation. It is vital to be honest and write down everything that arises for you without judgment.

October 10, 2020

Today I am sitting with Lepidolite and my feelings of stress and anxiety. I feel overwhelmed by balancing all of the extra responsibilities on my shoulders due to the coronavirus pandemic. It just seems to be coming to a head finally. Business, homeschooling, extra precautions when running errands, not spending time with my mom and my friends, trying to still connect with my family and grow as a person. It's just so much.

As I sit with this during my session, it feels like a mild headache, a tightening in my shoulders, and this tight hot ball of stress just below my ribcage. I feel the weight of this year bearing down heavily on me. I want to cry, but I hold it in, trying to be the strong, supportive rock for the family. I have been trying to soldier on since March and not waste energy hoping that it would end soon so we can go back to "normal." I can no longer ignore that I can't just bear everything, all the time, anymore.

When I ask to hear more about this stress and anxiety, I hear, "This is too much." It's such a short phrase and I even wonder if it's my own pity or despair. But it feels so kind and loving to me. "This is too much." When I ask, "What do I need to improve this?" I am advised that I need to let some expectations go, set them free. And to find a way to reserve one day a week to relax. No chores or errands. The whole family should relax together. I don't know if I can do that, but we'll see. I sat and breathed for a few extra minutes today to allow the Lepidolite to melt the sensation of stress and send it down into the earth. To take all this tension that I don't need. And I feel some ease.

After a second session, I am noticing that the sensations of stress have changed. I write down decisions I have made to manage this challenge.

October 18, 2020

Today is my day with Lepidolite. The stress about responsibilities and expectations is still with me. Today it feels like a dull but persistent pressure surrounding my body. It's not so intense as last week. I feel a little more numb and less like I'll split open. I have decided to let go of some of my business offerings for a time. This may not be a permanent change, but a need to set some things to the side to make more space for peace in my life and not be so pressured.

When I asked today to tell me more about my stress, I hear, "It's a good start." I guess this means that I have more work to do. I have decided to carve out Saturdays for family relaxation. I'll have to move those errands and chores to another day, but I really want to try and give it a shot. When I ask what I need, "A day of rest," and I see a great big pink heart in my mind. My Lepidolite is also in the shape of a heart. I immediately feel this is about giving myself a break and not being so hard on myself. We are all doing the best we can. I choose to give myself some love.

After the third session, I note a sense of even more freedom from my stress and anxiety. I now have a plan in place to create more peace and balance in my life.

October 24, 2020

This is Lepidolite day to sit with my stress. I am feeling much, much lighter in my body when considering my daily life stress. When I look at this in my body, there is still a loose knot in my torso's core, but it's more open, less heavy. I also get the impression of a breeze over my body, like I am actually feeling lighter like the wind. When I ask to tell me more, I hear, "You are doing enough. Don't let the doubt trip you up." And truthfully, I have been feeling a bit "lazy" by doing less and spending some time resting, but I need to give that inner critic, that source of stress and doubt, a rest. But if I'm being honest with myself, I do tend to feel a sense of pride in being productive. I even try to be efficient and productive with my hobbies. I don't often give myself time to just sit and "be." It makes me feel lazy. And maybe I really need to address these issues so I can ease off my need to be "doing" and just enjoy some time "being."

When I ask what I need, I just feel freedom and relief. After a Saturday of not having so many responsibilities, I just knew this is exactly what I needed. I need to keep up this Sacred Saturday, as I am now calling it. I can't tell you how great I felt on Sunday after a day of planned relaxation. I was motivated, enthusiastic, and was super productive. A day "off" actually helped me get more work done this week because I was excited about what I had planned. Yes!

I may have been able to notice these changes and improvements from my own memory, but it was so much clearer and undeniable when I would read back over my own words and feelings. When writing, try to remain free from editing, correcting, or judging your experience as you write. Just allow the words to flow. Let it be raw, straight from your heart and experience. Don't worry about spelling, grammar, or punctuation. Just write. And when you feel done, then take a slow, deep breath and close your book.

CHAPTER 12

Developing Spontaneous Practices

I hope you feel curious and excited about starting your daily practices. These will form the foundation for inner reflection on your major support needs and begin the process of transformation and change in your life. That is the beginning. Spontaneous practices are those quick moments that will help you directly during the "heat of the moment" life challenges. Both approaches work hand-in-hand to help us live more aware, intentional, and joyous days.

Know What Situations to Look For

Unlike the daily practices, you won't know which exercises you'll be performing on a given day. Instead, you'll use your list of emotions and situations that you prepared for your daily practices to guide you. It will be your challenge to stay aware of these occurrences and be ready for practice. Pay close attention to your emotions and thoughts during your daily activities. Keep your Guardian Gemstones nearby for quick use. You might need them once a day or 10 times. There is no limit. If you need them, use them. The more you use them, the quicker you'll feel the effects of the practice take place when you pick up the stone. It will be important to know and look for the guideposts that your identified life situations may display. Also, plan what you will need in that moment—to release, invite, or just be.

Recognizing When the Situation Arises

This may seem like obvious guidance, but as I was just getting started with my own practice, I would often not be able to see that I was in the midst of a stress attack until it had been hours and I finally asked myself, "Why I have been so snappy with everyone today? Ohhhhh, I'm stressed out about my test tomorrow." There are several guideposts and symptoms we can look for to notice when one of our life situations has triggered us: the situation itself, our emotions, and our body signals.

If we are lucky, we can identify right away a situation that is going to need support. That interview you are doing tomorrow, the event both you and your ex need to attend, the doctor appointment, sitting down to write, and wanting inspiration—anything that you can see coming. We can plan ahead for these situations by making sure we have that gemstone nearby and that we are prepared to sit, maybe multiple times, leading up to or during the event.

The second guidepost is to feel the emotions. This is a practice that really creates an environment of mindfulness and attention that can eventually work in our favor. Pay attention to how you're feeling all day long. Frequently check in with your heart and mind to see what's going on. You may be working on a project and find yourself being critical about the work you're producing. This judgment then acts as a signal to remind you that you wanted support from your Inner Guide to reduce self-criticism. Then you know it's time to sit with Rose Quartz and invite in some self-compassion. Find yourself feeling nervous? Take a moment to examine why. Have a work meeting coming up? Oh, that's right, inviting more confidence at work was one of the life situations. Time to sit with the Citrine.

Finally, being in tune with your body can help you recognize physical symptoms that tell you that you need to pay attention. This may take some time and awareness to start associating physical symptoms with a situation, but it can be a powerful indicator. That tightness in your stomach, low-grade headache, shoulder tension, lower back pain, and much more can all be physical messages and manifestations of emotion.

Often, these emotions and physical sensations are something you have been starting to notice during your daily meditations. Your daily journal can help you identify the symptoms that arise with each life situation. Knowing these will help you plan even better day after day and week after week. The quicker you notice you need a spontaneous practice, the quicker the gemstones will be able to improve the quality of your days.

Sit with Your Gemstones When You Need Support

Once you notice you need support, it's important to take some time as soon as you can, wherever you are, and sit with your gemstone and your feelings. You do not need a special place to sit or a formal practice for these in-the-moment practices. They also don't need to be that long. This is meant to be a support in your life, not a burden or intrusion. Also, the more you practice, the faster you will feel the support arrive for you.

When the need arises and you see it, find the gemstone you have identified to support that need. Sit down somewhere as quiet as you can find. This is not always possible if you find yourself overwhelmed in a retail store, but the practice can absolutely be done right there in the store. Hold your stone, start taking some slow deep breaths, and allow yourself to feel the situation. If you don't know the trigger of the emotion, ask yourself, "Tell me more about this emotion I'm feeling." Listen for your Inner Guide to provide some insight. Maybe you'll learn more about the trigger and be able to prepare yourself ahead of time.

Then perform the intention to release, invite, or just be. Several situations will be eased by releasing some thought, emotion, or physical sensation. This is often the case with anxiety, frustration, regret, jealousy, fear, or any emotion or thought cycle we want to let go of. In your spontaneous practice, take a slow, deep breath in and allow the sensation to float away on your exhale. It may take many breathes to start feeling the relief. Breathe in and exhale fear out until eventually you feel stable once more. The more you practice this with your gemstone, the faster the release will occur until it is almost instantaneous after you pick up the stone.

Other situations are supported by inviting in a specific quality, such as inspiration, confidence, love, energy, passion, or some benefit we want to cultivate more of in life. For the spontaneous practice, sit with your gemstone, imagine a bright white light in front of you that holds the quality you need. As you inhale, slowly take in and absorb this light within you. Repeat this as long as you need until the feeling starts to grow within you. Breathe in the quality, exhale, and let it settle into your body until eventually you feel uplifted and ready.

Then sometimes we need to *just be*. We need to take a quiet moment to settle, get centered and grounded, and bring ourselves into the present moment. This could be when we feel overwhelmed, scattered, or just need to take a breath so we can figure out the next step. The spontaneous practice will be just sitting with your Guardian Gemstone and bringing your attention to the sensation of breathing. How does it feel to breathe right now? Feel the support of the solid, stable earth beneath you. Know that you are sitting on top of the entire planet, directly over its center, and you have access to all of the energy of the earth. Just breathe, sitting solidly on this earth.

If you've had any significant insights, you may want to take a few moments, if life allows, to record them in your journal. If you are in a crowded place, you can do this practice standing in line at a store or even at a party. You don't even need to close your eyes. Just find your stone, hold it, feel your inner messages, and breathe. You can release, invite, or just be without anyone around you noticing.

Sample Spontaneous Practice

Green Aventurine is a stone that I often use to help me have more patience. I often get frustrated with situations out of my control. Patience is, ultimately, our ability to sit and be with situations we cannot control—waiting for test results, that my kids won't stop fighting, or that I don't have enough time to finish something that day. If impatience is starting to rise, I tend to start feeling that sense of inner constriction and tightness with an eventual growl of frustration. These are emotional and physical symptoms I have noticed within myself that I stay alert for. When I notice these, I pick up my Aventurine, find the quietest place to sit, close my eyes, and breathe. I allow myself to feel the emotions of impatience and to bring to mind the situation causing frustration. I remind myself that I cannot control it, that this impatience is not helping and is only causing me suffering. In this situation, I need to release the frustration. As I exhale, I allow the sensations to drift away on my breath. It may take a few minutes, but the impatience does dissipate. Rather than acting out of frustration and potentially taking it out on others or stewing about it all day, I have intentionally let it go and can move on with my day with a more peaceful heart and mind.

Sample Complete Crystal Wisdom Practice

Here is an example of how this full practice may look for someone. My client, whom I will call Lisa, had chosen a few areas of her heart and life that she'd like support with. She had recently broken up with a long-term boyfriend and was feeling heartache and low self-worth. She regularly came home feeling moody and irritable due to negative, competitive coworkers. Lisa had also been having some difficulty sleeping at night. She chooses Rose Quartz to support her heart healing, Black Tourmaline to help her cope with a hostile environment, and Amazonite to help her sleep. Each of these gemstones and life situations is clearly written down on one page in her journal.

During her daily practices, she sits with her heartache one day, work environment the next, and sleeplessness on the third day, then back to her heart healing to continue this rotation. Lisa journals each day, noticing where the source of her relationship pain is, where she needs to provide herself with more self-love, what is most triggering at work, and what seems to be preventing her from sleeping. She takes notes of how she feels not only when she is in those situations but also when she reflects on them in meditation.

For spontaneous practices, she knows she'll need the Rose Quartz during those occasions she has to interact with her ex (because they share mutual friends) and when she is struck by loneliness and self-judgment. She plans to release pain and heartache about her ex and invite in self-compassion and tenderness for herself. Lisa keeps a piece of Black Tourmaline on her work desk to be available when she notices herself in a bad mood due to coworkers' gossiping and negative attitudes. She plans to release frustration or to just be as she feels appropriate. Then at night, she'll sit with Amazonite before bed to help calm and soothe her overactive mind for sleep. She will breathe out the swirling thoughts and invite in-body relaxation.

Over time, she realizes that she is no longer triggered when her ex-boyfriend is around. She has stopped judging and blaming herself for the breakup. Lisa realizes this was not a healthy relationship that was going to support her in the long run. Rose Quartz has served a valuable role in her life in healing her heart, and she feels it has served its purpose. Lisa has decided to bring Honey Calcite into her Guardian Gemstone team to help her build the confidence she wants to develop her skills and interview for a promotion. Rose Quartz will now take an honored place on her crystal shelf and still be there on the occasion that her heart needs a hug.

CHAPTER 13

Maintaining Your
Crystal Wisdom Life

Now you are ready to begin your journey to a brighter and more peaceful life! One in which you move through your days with attention and intention. Even when life throws you curveballs during the day, you can still react to them with wisdom and thoughtfulness. You will see your life challenges shrink away and no longer have a grip on you as they have before. The rapids of life will no longer bash you against the river edges, but you will flow with them like an expert river rafter—moving your body and paddling in just the right way to keep you upright and moving down the river with excitement and courage. This is what Crystal Wisdom will unlock for you.

Practice Daily

The Crystal Wisdom practice results will depend on the time, energy, and dedication you put into it. It is vital that you reserve some time every day for sitting with your chosen moments to give them attention and honor. It is only with regular reflection and practice in releasing, inviting, and being that you will start seeing the results of your practice. This Crystal Wisdom practice is a skill that anyone can develop. You don't need any special certifications or talents. You only need the desire to look deeply at your life and to keep coming back to this inner space over and over again. Your skill at tapping into your inner wisdom and managing daily life situations will strengthen and be more effective in time. Your ability to engage with your chosen life challenges will become more natural and cause less suffering. But only if you have a regular practice.

Looking at your amount of stress, self-judgment, or desire to be creative just once a week is not enough for transformation to take root. But this also does not require many hours a day—20 minutes a day for your daily practice and a few minutes each time an identified situation arises. These minutes a day add up, day after day, to sustained and focused effort, creating change in your life. The more often you engage with a challenging situation, the easier it will become and the quicker you will be able to take action. The more often you sit with the situation, the sooner you will figure out the root cause of the challenge and start initiating a concrete resolution.

Coming back to this inner space and inner wisdom for guidance will shine the light on the truth of the matter and highlight the best path for you to travel. So, take the time, sit and reflect, even when you don't feel like it. Some of my most potent insights have come when I didn't feel like sitting in my practice that day because my "trying to figure it out" part of my brain wasn't engaged. I was just resting with my gemstone and the wisdom arrived. The more often you sit, the more opportunities for insights to arise, so practice, practice, practice.

Reflect and Celebrate

Every few weeks, I recommend reading through your journal to see how your situations and daily life have been evolving. In the hustle of everyday life, it may not be apparent that change or improvements are happening, but if you sit down to read over your previous entries, it is much easier to see how your heart, body, and mind have been responding to your practice. If you notice that a particular area of your life has improved, take some time to celebrate! Hurray! Your focus and dedication to your own inner work have started to yield fruit. The transformation is happening. You don't have to wait for enormous life change to celebrates the wins. If you are able to dissolve that frustration quicker than you usually do, this is great. If you notice you are starting to be kinder to yourself, wonderful! Take a moment to sit and feel some gratitude for the improvement and appreciation for doing the work to get you there.

You may want to set up a celebration plan ahead of time. Decide what might make a joyful moment to appreciate the hard work. Maybe buy a luxurious new tea to enjoy, pick a new gemstone to buy, spend some time outdoors breathing in the fresh air, or listen to a song that represents success. Take a moment to pick up your gemstone and send it gratitude and thanks for its role in improving your life.

Reevaluate Your Guardian Gemstone Team

As your practice is more established, you will find that you'll be reaching for a gemstone less frequently over time. Daily practices with that stone may seem more peaceful and bring up less emotion or evoke a sense of accomplishment. In fact, during one of your daily sessions, you may receive the guidance that your work with that gemstone is complete. When you notice any one of these occurrences, then it's time to sit in meditation with that gemstone and see if your need for that crystal has been completed. If so, this is a major cause for celebration! A challenge, transition, or opportunity has been accomplished and it's time to give that gemstone a little rest.

Take a few moments to thank your gemstone for its support and hard work enabling you to improve your life. It has been your partner during a challenging time in your life and has helped you transform. This gemstone can be placed wherever you are storing the rest of your crystal collection. You may still need it on occasion as lingering emotion arises, but it can take its place with your backup team of crystals.

When a Guardian is transitioned out of your team, it is an excellent time to sit and reevaluate your life needs. Head on back to Chapter 5 and walk through the steps again to see if there is a new situation you want support with or another gemstone calling to speak to you. This is a practice that should be performed every 2–3 months. Life changes. What might be top-of-mind in one season is no longer so urgent during the next. Over the course of several years working with this Crystal Wisdom practice, I notice a dramatic shift in my team year over year. One year, I may be very focused on preparing for a significant life transition. The next year, the change is complete, and I am working to build up a new part of my life. This is natural. Your current Guardian Gemstone team should reflect your life right now, in the present moment. This is how we make progress and initiate actual life changes.

CHAPTER 14

Common Crystal Questions

As you move along in your journey of Crystal Wisdom, different situations and questions may arise as you practice. I am taking this chapter as an opportunity to provide some answers to the most common questions I receive as a Crystal Educator.

Why are there multiple stones for a particular quality?

Each individual gemstone often supports a dozen or more aspects of life. Initially, this is part of what makes the practice of crystal energy world so confusing and complicated. What gemstone do I actually need? Flipping through an alphabetized book of crystals makes it difficult to narrow down which gemstones support specific life situations. However, if you use the Crystal Wisdom practice, it makes this process so much easier.

Ultimately, the fact that many, many gemstones support sleep works in our favor. What if the only gemstone that helped us sleep was Amethyst? And what if you didn't feel particularly attracted to Amethyst, the color purple, or the Quartz family in general? Then you would not feel connected enough to your gemstone for the practice to work effectively. It would work, but much slower since you don't have the enthusiasm and relationship with the stone to accelerate the process. Instead, there are so many gemstones that support sleep and you can choose just the right crystal that you feel strongly drawn to. Howlite, Amazonite, Moonstone, Lepidolite, and so many more will help you sleep. In fact, the different gemstones actually support various nuances of sleep. For example, multiple crystals can help calm a busy mind, relax the body, ward away nightmares, or even feel secure in your bed at night.

When you are trying to locate your Guardian Gemstones, don't just go with the first gemstone you find to help you with, say, creativity. Identify as many gemstones as possible for creativity and then see which one attracts you the most. The more intense your attraction to a gemstone, the more effective it will be for you during meditation.

What about physical healing?

Crystal books often list the physical symptoms that can be resolved through crystal healing. That is outside of the scope of this Crystal Wisdom practice. For physical healing requests, I combine gemstones with my Reiki practice to aid the energy of the Reiki. That practice is called Crystal Reiki. The Crystal Wisdom practice supports our inner wisdom space. However, I will say that when someone eases emotional, mental, and spiritual wounds, they are in a much better energetic environment to heal injuries and illnesses.

If you sprain your ankle but are still working long hours, running excessive errands, eating unhealthily, and staying up late, that is not conducive for healing. If, instead, you took the day off work, sat and put your foot up with ice and warm compresses, ate well, stay hydrated, and got plenty of sleep, your ankle is likely to heal a lot faster. Same with Crystal Wisdom. If your energy is flowing smoothly, you are not carrying so much stress, your heart aches less, and you live with optimism and joy, you have set the stage for an improved healing experience.

For example, reduced stress and anxiety will often lower blood pressure or relieve tension headaches. Getting better sleep will help you recover from a cold faster. Heal the mind, heart, and spirit and the body will follow.

Is it okay to gift gemstones?

Some people feel that because crystal energy work can be a very personal practice, giving someone a crystal they didn't request may be an intrusion. I believe it all comes down to intention. Giving the gift of gemstones is a beautiful and thoughtful gift. Some of my most cherished gemstones have been a gift from someone else. They happened to give me just the right gemstone to lift me up when I needed it. They didn't have that intention, but the Universe guided them to the perfect crystal. If you decide to give someone a gemstone, make sure it is done with no ulterior motives. Don't give a crystal because you want the person to change. There is a difference between giving someone a gemstone to help them through a difficult time of loss, pain, or grief and giving one because you'd like them to be more patient, focused, or organized. Make sure it is done with *their* Highest Good in mind, not yours. If you feel called to send someone a particular stone, then do so. Maybe the Universe is using you as a channel to assist them. They will receive from it what they need.

What if I feel overwhelmed by a crystal during practice?

This can absolutely happen, especially if you are working on deep emotional wounds, major life transitions, or intense triggers. If you feel overwhelmed during your daily practice, set your gemstone aside and just breathe. It is often helpful to have a grounding stone nearby, like Hematite, Black Tourmaline, or Smoky Quartz, to help you touch back into the earth's deeply supportive energy.

Don't worry if this happens; it is entirely normal. When facing large issues in our lives, we can sometimes be hit with a wave of emotion. This is not a sign that you are not ready to face the problem. If you feel drawn to working with it, then you are ready. But it may take more time and self-compassion in the first few weeks. Be gentle with yourself. Have friends and family to contact if you need to talk. Plan some self-care to nurture yourself during this time. Good coffee or tea, hot showers or baths, taking time out in nature, nice candles, your favorite music, or a good book. After the overwhelming moment has passed, send appreciation and gratitude to yourself for the courage to sit with it, even if briefly, and then take some time with self-care.

What if my gemstone cracks or breaks?

Accidents do happen. One day you may drop a gemstone and it cracks or completely breaks in two. Will the crystal still work? Do you need to replace it? And what do you do with the original piece(s)? I assure you that cracks and breaks do not inhibit a crystal's ability to provide you with support in your practice. Consider that all gemstones in your collection have been broken off from their much more extensive source to be sold to collectors. Also, most gemstones already have internal cracks and inclusions. It's also very rare to purchase polished stones without some surface chips or flaws. This is the natural state of gemstones. Each one is unique and has internal flaws, and flawless material is actually quite expensive.

You are not looking for perfection with your gemstone choice but attraction.

That said, what if you drop your gemstone and it cracks? If the crack doesn't bother you in the slightest, then continue using it. If it does feel like it disrupts the relationship you have and is interfering with your practice, then buy a new one. The cracked one can be used as a backup if you feel you could benefit from having a gemstone in reserve to take to another location. It can also be gifted to someone else. The other person will not know that the gemstone looked differently before, so the crack won't influence them.

If the gemstone breaks in two, then you now have two gemstones—hurray! Again, if this bothers you, get a new stone and reserve or gift the broken ones. Some people feel that you should bury the broken pieces back into the earth, but I don't feel it's necessary. To me, gifting it to others feels more appropriate, but proceed as you feel called to do so.

Some people have reported that their gemstone mysteriously cracked overnight. Is this an omen of bad luck? No. Remember, gemstones often have existing internal cracks. A temperature change may cause the stone to crack even more. During the evening, the temperature lowers and then rises again the next day. The larger the temperature difference, the more likely this is to occur. This is especially common if the stones are left on a windowsill at night or near a heater or fireplace. Sometimes the heat of one's hand may cause more fragile crystals, like Calcite, to crack while in your hand. This is perfectly natural.

Another frequent question I receive is: It is okay to glue the pieces back together? Only if it won't disrupt your connection and relationship to the stone. Sometimes people buy pyramids, obelisks, or towers online and the tip breaks off in shipping. I think it's entirely appropriate to glue the little tip back on, very carefully, with some glue.

Which gemstones will fade in the sunlight?

It is important to know which gemstones will fade in bright sunlight so you can find a different method to charge them. Using Reiki or moonlight is much safer for these stones. Avoid placing these gemstones in direct sunlight, on windowsills, anyplace where light will shine on them by a window, or even when wearing them on bright summer days.

All colors of the translucent Quartz family will fade in sunlight. This includes Amethyst, Rose Quartz, Smoky Quartz, and Citrine. Fluorite is a common crystal that you might have in tumbled or rough form that will fade. The beautiful multicolored Fluorite is one you definitely want to protect from sunlight. Gemstones you might have in jewelry form that fade are Aquamarine and Sapphires. Opal will dry out and crack in the sunlight, so take extra care with it.

Finally, these gemstones are commonly purchased for crystal energy work and they should be protected from the sun: Apatite, Amazonite, Calcite, Kunzite, Morganite, Sodalite, and Pink or Red Tourmaline. There are additional gemstones that are sun-sensitive but are not found in tumbled form very often.

Should I avoid putting certain gemstones in water?

In my experience with tumbling and polishing gemstones, I have found that there are very few stones that will be damaged in water. Rock tumbling involves letting stones tumble in a mixture of water and grit to smooth out the surface and prepare it to receive a polish. Some gemstones are softer and should only be tumbled for a brief time, but they are not damaged by the water itself. It's the tumbling and grit that cause the stone to wear down, not the water.

Given this context, washing a crystal or gemstone for a few minutes in water or a brief rainstorm will not harm it. Gemstones that are quickly water-soluble are not commonly used as crystal healing gemstones, and they often require you to soak the gemstone in water for hours.

Some people like to soak their gemstones in water, but this could damage certain gemstones' polish or cause iron-based ones to rust. Avoid soaking the following stones: Amber, Angelite, Calcite, Celestite, Fluorite, Hematite, Jade, Lapis, Lazuli, Lepidolite, Lodestone, Magnetite, Malachite, and Shungite.

How do I handle potentially toxic gemstones?

Most gemstones contain minerals that, when concentrated, can be toxic. These minerals are arsenic, asbestos, barium, borate, copper, lead, nickel, silicosis, and more. There are hundreds of gemstones that contain these minerals in some quantity. However, do not be afraid! The danger from these gemstones comes primarily when they are cut or soaked in water. Gemstone cutters should be aware of potentially dangerous gemstones and wear appropriate safety gear so they don't breathe in the particulates.

There are very few gemstones that are dangerous even to touch and you will not accidentally run across them in rock stores. You may encounter them at gemstone expos and conventions because geological societies often have obscure specimens available for sale. It has been my experience that these toxic gemstones are very clearly labeled with warning signs and the booth owners will handle them with gloves.

It is a good practice to wash your hands after holding gemstones for more than a few minutes. After your daily or spontaneous practice, give your hands a quick wash. The sweat on our hands may combine with any rough parts of the stones and leave a residue. This will not be immediately harmful if you forget. It will take consistent periods of ingestion to feel the effects of trace toxins. If you get into the practice of washing your hands afterward, then you'll be safer overall. Fluorite, Malachite, Galena, and Bumblebee Jasper are a few stones with which you should have a more diligent handwashing routine.

Should I consume crystal elixirs? NO!

This question immediately follows the previous question for a reason. Even mildly toxic gemstones soaked in water can be dangerous when ingested! For this reason, I never recommend putting gemstones directly in water and consuming it. Never. This is a dangerous practice. There are products that can make the practice of crystal elixirs safe. There are water bottles that are created with cavities in the bottom and a screw-on base. These bottles allow you to place crystals in the cavity, screw on the base, and fill the bottle with water while keeping the crystals completely separate from the water. This is a safe practice. You can infuse the water with the energy of the gemstones without potentially contaminating your water.

I also would not recommend putting gemstones directly in bath water because your skin can absorb the toxins in the water. If you want to bathe with gemstones in your bath water, just put them in a Ziploc bag, zip it tightly shut, and place the bag in the water.

Are there any negative stones? Or stones I shouldn't work with?

There are people who believe that some crystals are inherently negative and that you should avoid using them unless you want to be plagued with nightmares, bad luck, and negativity. I don't agree with this at all. I have never encountered any gemstone that I felt had an inherently negative energy within it that would attract more negativity. All gemstones come from the loving and healing earth. None of them, not even the highly toxic ones, are full of bad intent. I do believe that someone may not be ready to work with a particular gemstone. They might be overwhelmed by its effects if not prepared.

If you are working with a stone that encourages the opposite of what you need for a situation, you will feel uncomfortable. You may be working with high-energy stones because you feel lethargic and tired during the day, but what you actually need are stones that encourage better rest and sleep. It will feel like you are relying on coffee to compensate for poor sleep. You'll feel jittery, unfocused, and eventually exhausted from a caffeine crash. Make sure that during the Guardian identification process you are genuinely looking at what you need in life. Sit with a situation, look at it from all angles, and ensure that you're treating the root cause rather than a symptom.

Some gemstones, such as Obsidian, Malachite, and Lapis Lazuli, encourage you to look at issues you've been avoiding. They are stones of honest truth. This can be quite uncomfortable if you are not prepared for it. If you are attracted to one of these stones, you probably need to explore some underlying issues, but it is best to prepare and understand what you may experience beforehand. Other stones like Oynx and Leopardskin Jasper facilitate shadow work, which may be uncomfortable if you are not emotionally ready to look at the dark spaces. Before choosing a gemstone, read up on all of its supportive qualities so that you are not surprised by something unexpected.

Does my spiritual belief system prevent me from practicing Crystal Wisdom?

Absolutely not. This is a process of mindfulness and inner exploration that is compatible with any religious or spiritual practice. Gemstones are meant to support you in your daily life but are not intended to replace any spiritual presence or practice you hold dear. They do not attract negativity. They are creations directly from the earth and represent that pure, natural source. You can even ask for assistance and guidance from whichever presence you consider divine during your daily and spontaneous practices. It is highly encouraged that you engage all sources of wisdom and guidance to aid your personal reflections on your life challenges.

Can I combine certain gemstones?

Yes, you absolutely can. The deeper your Crystal Wisdom practice, the more you will be familiar with certain stones' energy and benefits. You'll learn how certain gemstones amplify or complement other ones. You may intuit certain combinations that seem to work well for you. I tend to use both Green Aventurine and Howlite for patience and I use Sunstone and Hematite for social gatherings and public speaking. As your practice becomes more established and you get to know more and more stones, you will experience this, too.

When asked if someone should combine a particular set of stones, I always say to ask yourself first, "What is my intention for these gemstones?" Do you want to combine Rose Quartz and Amethyst to strengthen your intuition regarding love? Then this is a great match. If your intention for them is to protect you from negative energy, then this isn't the right combination. If you don't know what you want from that particular combination of gemstones, then you won't be able to identify if you're receiving the benefits or not. If you want to wear them together and want to know if they "cancel each other out," that is outside of the scope of Crystal Wisdom. This is a practice that works with specific, declared intentions. If you have separate intentions and practices for Onyx and Carnelian and you want to wear them simultaneously, you can do that. You will receive the support of both in their respective areas.

If you find yourself really drawn to two gemstones together and you don't know why, follow the process laid out in Chapter 5. Look up the supportive benefits of both gemstones, write down the qualities that stand out to you side by side, and see where they might complement each other. Does this seem relevant to your life? Then this could be what your gemstones were calling to you for. You might consider developing a practice that uses both stones to support that area of your life.

Can I use orgonite or crystal grids during my practice?

Orgonite is an object created by encasing metals and gemstones in resin to amplify and focus their energies. They often come in the shape of pyramids but are made as discs and pendants as well. Often these are used to boost the energy of a gemstone within a room. Crystal grids are created from many gemstones in an intentional geometric design and are intended to fill a space with that energy. While both of these gemstone creations can add additional gemstone energy to your home or office, they are outside the scope of Crystal Wisdom. If you are working with Rose Quartz and one of your Guardian Gemstones, you should have a piece you can hold in your hand and make skin contact with. However, you can use orgonite and crystal grids to keep that Rose Quartz energy awake and flowing throughout your house to enhance your inner work.

What if I want to attract money and wealth?

This is easily the most common question I receive about crystal energy work. Unfortunately, there is no "get rich quick" crystal. There are gemstones that will help you recognize new opportunities, have the courage to advance your career, motivate you to learn and prepare for a new career, or help you organize your finances. Yellow and Golden gemstones are very supportive in this area. They boost motivation, confidence, courage, and drive to go out and do what needs to be done to create life situations that will bring in more abundance. But gemstones won't boost your luck or help you win the lotto.

If you feel that financial issues are a big struggle in your life, ask your Inner Guide more about this during your daily practice. This is a life challenge that really needs to be examined at its source. Do you feel afraid to apply for that promotion? Do you have difficulties budgeting? Would you like to switch careers but need the motivation to prepare for the change? Maybe you are doing fine financially but fear scarcity. Or perhaps you're not recognizing and accepting new opportunities when they arise. There are many reasons why we can feel a lack of abundance in life, but life change won't happen without honesty and work. Crystal Wisdom will help to reveal the truth within us. It is then up to us to do the work that will bring more financial stability.

CHAPTER 15

Living Life with Crystal Wisdom

Do the Crystal Wisdom practices make your life perfect? No. It will not shield you from the turbulence and challenges in life or the heartbreaks and disappointments. But it does improve your ability to respond wisely and mindfully to both the stressors and the opportunities in life. As you gather and work with your team of Guardian Gemstones and cultivate a regular Crystal Wisdom practice to support you in your life, you will feel less buffeted by the high winds and feel more flight and flow with the wind currents. Life will feel a little less like a struggle and more like a changing landscape that you have the skills and tools to adapt to.

When you begin to trust the power of your gemstones and your inner wisdom to guide you, you may find yourself feeling like your days are fuller, more productive, and filled with more joys than before. That is because you are paying attention to your life and your inner reactions to it. You are noticing emotions and situations before you react, and you can mindfully choose how to proceed. There are additional side benefits to paying such close attention. You soak in the pleasure of watching your child play in the sand. You notice the moment the spring flowers start to bloom in your yard. You genuinely enjoy and savor that first delicious bite of a dessert. You take moments to just sit, breathe, and notice the world around you. I wish many flavors of these moments for you. Through the Crystal Wisdom practice, I hope you find that space of joy, peace, and resiliency that will brighten all the rest of the moments of your life.

Shannon Marie

Shannon Marie is supported in life by her husband, children, and their cuddly cats in a home full of gemstones. She has spent the last 15 years creating gemstone jewelry, writing articles about crystals, and providing meditation and gemstone education videos on YouTube. After many years of informal study, Shannon became a Certified Professional Gemologist with the International Gem Society.

Shannon's extensive studies of therapeutic healing modalities began with a certification as a Reiki Master and Teacher in 2004. She then went on to obtain a master's degree from the Institute of Transpersonal Psychology, a 200-hour Yoga Teacher Training course with Blue Lotus Yoga in North Carolina, and a Practitioner Certification in Phoenix Rising Yoga Therapy. She enjoys meditation with her Buddhist sangha at Dawn Mountain in Houston, Texas. Shannon combines her love and knowledge of gemstones with her broad scope of therapeutic training to create the transformative meditation practice of Crystal Wisdom.

ADDITIONAL RESOURCES

Crystals and Gemstones

Frazier, Karen, *Crystals for Healing: The Complete Reference Guide.* Berkley, CA: Althea Press, 2015.

Hall, Judy. *The Crystal Bible (Volumes 1–3).* Blue Ash, OH: Walking Stick Press, 2003–2013.

Melody. *Love is in the Earth: A Kaleidoscope of Crystals.* Wheat Ridge: Earth-Love Publishing, 1995.

Murphy, Stacie. *Tumbled Stones Picture Books; Volume 13: Over 700 Gemstones by Color.* 2016.

Peschek-Bohmer, F. and Schrieber, G. *Healing Crystals and Gemstones: From Amethyst to Zircon.* Germany: Konecky & Konecky, 2002.

Raphaell, Katrina. *Crystal Enlightenment: The Transforming Properties of Crystals and Healing.* Santa Fe: Aurora Press, 1985.

Raphaell, Katrina. *Crystal Healing: The Therapeutic Application of Crystals and Stones.* Santa Fe: Aurora Press, 1987.

Schumann, Walter. *Gemstones of the World (Fifth Edition).* New York: Sterling, 2013.

Simmons, R. and Ahsian, N. *The Book of Stones, Revised Edition: Who They Are and What They Teach.* Berkley, CA: North Atlantic Books, 2005.

Numerology

DeLorey, Christine. *Life Cycles: Your Emotional Journey to Freedom and Happiness.* Hallandale Beach, FL: Osmos Books, 2000.

Jordan, Juno. *Numerology: The Romance in Your Name.* Camarillo, CA: DeVorss Publications, 1965.

Tunis, Sarahdawn. *Angel Numbers Mastery: Everything You Need to Know About Angel Numbers and What They Mean for You.* Lakewood, CO: 2018.

Color Psychology

Haller, Karen. *The Little Book of Colour: How to Use the Psychology of Colour to Transform Your Life.* UK: Penguin Life, 2019.

Ter Maximus, Mercurius. *Color Symbolism: A Study of the Psychology and Meaning Behind Colors.* Heill, 2019.

ACKNOWLEDGMENTS

I am so grateful for the love of my amazing husband, Jeff. His unconditional and unwavering support and encouragement have enabled me to reach for my dreams and create a life-passioned business I am so proud of.

My kids inspire me to be the most authentic and loving version of myself that I can possibly be. I want to show them that dreams and goals can be achieved and how beautiful it is to truly be your unique and amazing self. I love watching them blossom and can't wait to see their flowers in full bloom.

I am forever grateful that my mom and dad inspired within me a love and appreciation for gemstones. They also encouraged me to try whatever I felt inspired and curious to learn. Their love for me was clear and undeniable.

To Catherine Gregory, Nathan Joblin, and the team at Modern Wisdom Press: Thank you so much for the stable support, inspiration, coaxing, and encouragement that has brought this book to life. I could not have hoped for a better team to work with during this passion project.

THANK YOU, DEAR READER!

Thank you for taking the time to learn about the deeply personal practice of Crystal Wisdom. I feel honored that you have decided to explore this world of crystals and gemstones with me. I wish you all the best as you take your steps down the Crystal Wisdom path.

Continuing Support

www.crystal-wisdom.com
www.youtube.com/c/ReikiGemWellness

Keep checking in there to learn about
new books, online courses, and live workshops.

Printed in Great Britain
by Amazon

37903715R00089